PETER SHELTON

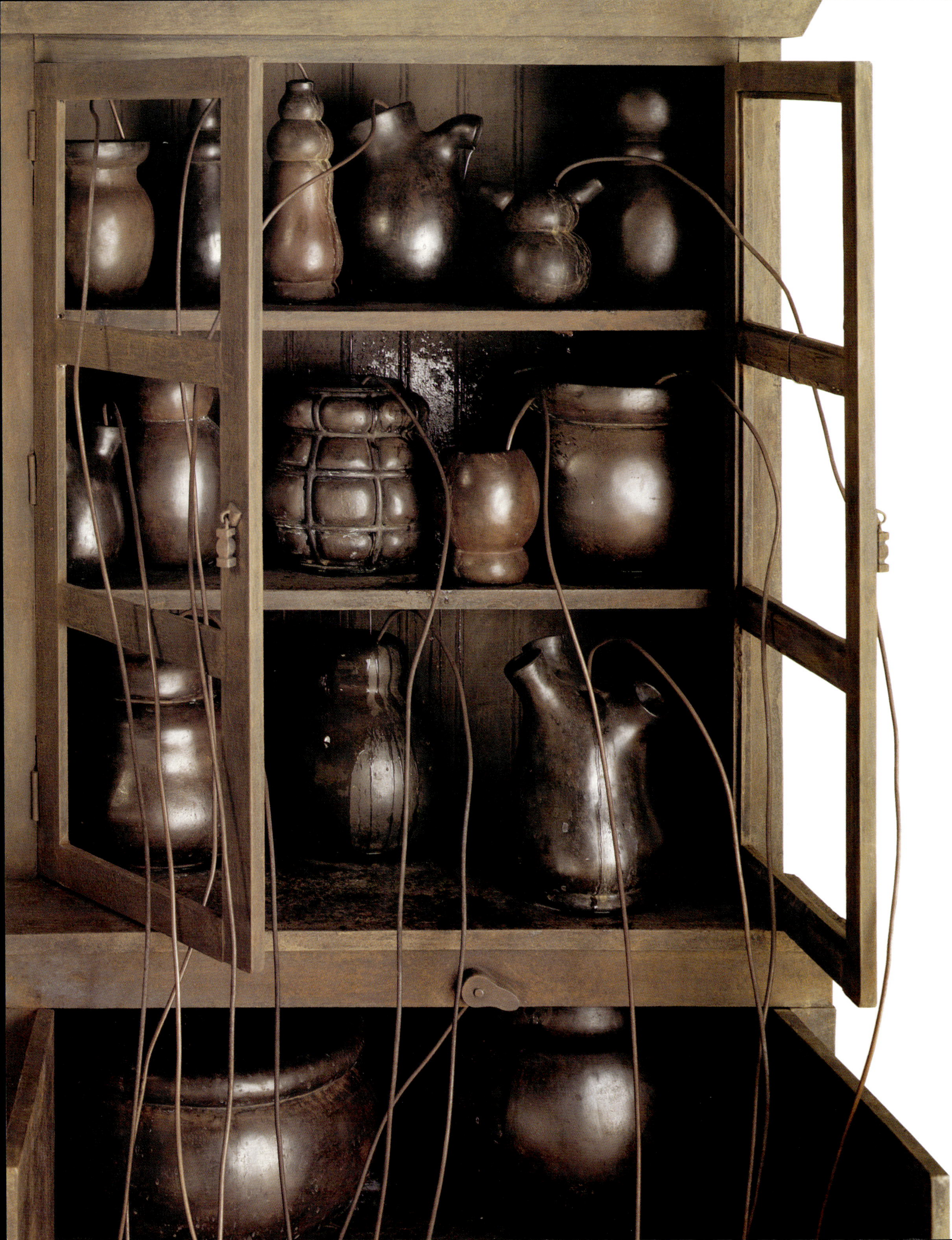

PETER SHELTON

bottlesbonesandthingsgetwet

Carol S. Eliel

LOS ANGELES COUNTY MUSEUM OF ART

Peter Shelton:
bottlesbonesandthingsgetwet
March 3–May 15, 1994

The exhibition was organized by the Los Angeles County Museum of Art and made possible through the generosity of the National Endowment for the Arts, Alice and Nahum Lainer, Robert and Mary Looker, Jack and Bonnie Wilke, Marshall and Doris Redman, and Merry Norris.

Published by the Los Angeles County Museum of Art, 5905 Wilshire Boulevard, Los Angeles, California 90036.

Library of Congress Catalog Card Number: 93-80887

ISBN 0-87587-170-4

Printed in the United States of America

Unless otherwise noted, all works illustrated are by Peter Shelton and are in the collection of the artist, courtesy of L.A. Louver, Venice, California.

Cover:
books, 1993
(detail)
from *thingsgetwet*, 1989–94

Frontispiece:
bowlshutch, 1993
(detail)
from *thingsgetwet*, 1989–94

Back cover:
horseheader, 1990–91
(detail)

Photo Credits

Unless otherwise indicated, all photographs are reproduced courtesy of the lenders. A complete list of works exhibited appears on pages 54–59.

Pat Bazelon, fig. 62

Peter Brenner, Los Angeles County Museum of Art, fig. 63

D. James Dee, figs. 2–4, 18–19, 43; pp. 6, 54, back cover

Brian Forrest, figs. 6, 52; pp. 55–56 (except *doublepoodleloopheader*)

Jay K. McNally, Los Angeles County Museum of Art, figs. 8–9, 25–26, 28–36, 38, 40–41, 44–46, 48–51, 53–55; front cover, frontispiece, pp. 10, 57–59, 72

Bill Orcutt, figs. 24, 57

Peter Shelton, figs. 1, 10–11, 16–17, 20, 22–23, 27, 47

Tom Vinetz, figs. 14–15, 21, 56

Daniel Zimbaldi, figs. 12–13

CONTENTS

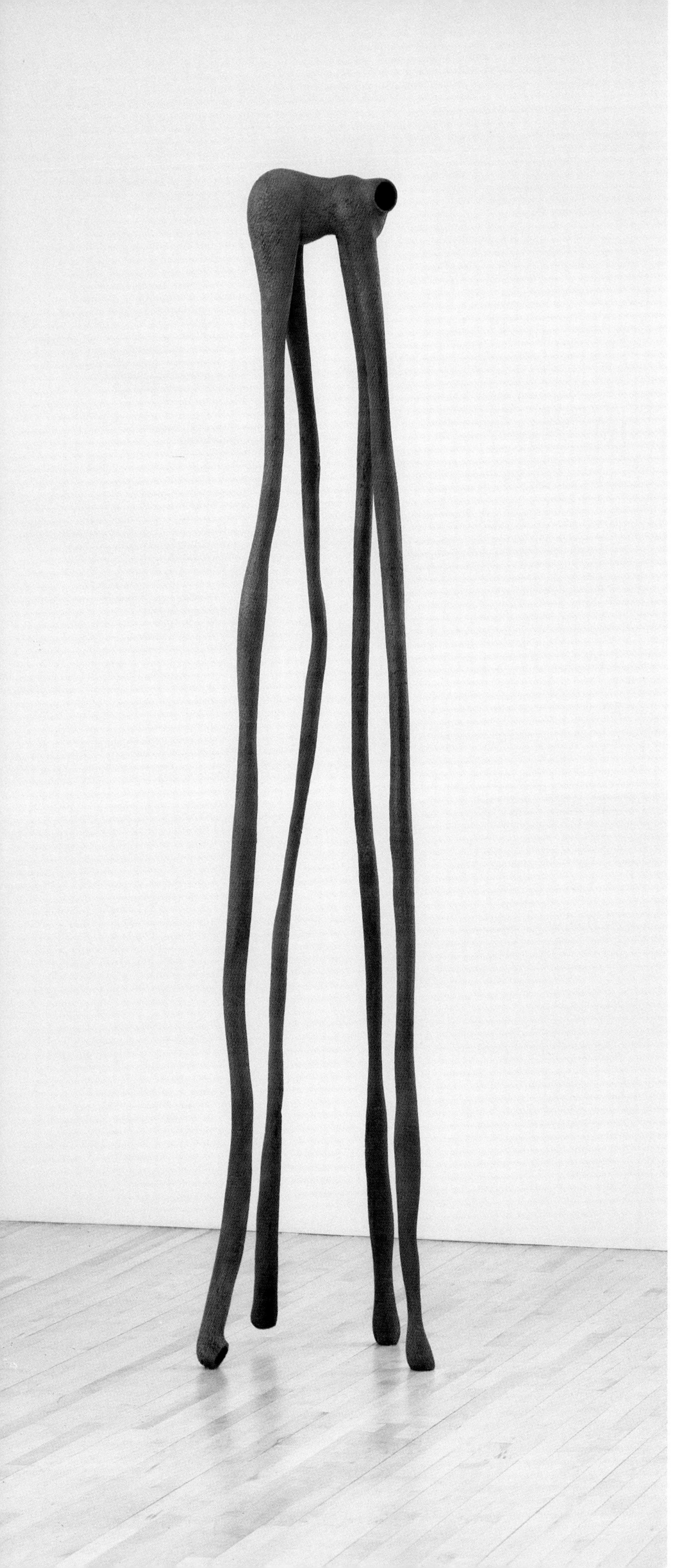

FOREWORD

fourleg, 1990–91
Bronze
119 x 24 x 22 in.
(302.3 x 61.7 x 55.9 cm)
Private collection

At a time when much contemporary sculpture is conceptual or deconstructive in nature, Peter Shelton is concerned with both form and meaning in his work. His sculptures, at times abstracted but never abstract, refer both to the human figure and to architecture (often simultaneously). A resident of Los Angeles and recipient in 1985 of the museum's Young Talent Purchase Award, sponsored by the department of twentieth-century art's Modern and Contemporary Art Council, Shelton is one of this country's most thought-provoking sculptors. In the nine years since the award Shelton's work has become increasingly ambitious as the artist has successfully challenged himself in terms of use of materials as well as scale and sculptural complexity. The richness of his work, which at first glance appears to be very easily readable and accessible, fully manifests itself to the viewer only after serious engagement and careful reflection.

This exhibition is an important component of the museum's ongoing program focusing on art of the present. Carol S. Eliel, associate curator of twentieth-century art, organized the exhibition. For her dedication to this show and for her thoughtful catalogue essay, which is the first comprehensive consideration of Shelton's work, we are most grateful. We are also appreciative of the National Endowment for the Arts and of the patrons and friends who so generously provided additional financial support for this exhibition. We are likewise indebted to the lenders to the exhibition who kindly allowed us to borrow work for the show. To all of them we offer our thanks for making this presentation possible.

The museum would also like to acknowledge Peter Shelton's contribution to this exhibition. We thank him for the sculptures themselves and for the many hours he graciously devoted to various organizational aspects of the show. His assistance and cooperation were key in bringing this project to fruition.

Stephanie Barron

Coordinator of curatorial affairs

ACKNOWLEDGMENTS

Peter Shelton's sculpture is a curator's dream: it both provides immediate visual gratification and further rewards slow and deliberate consideration. To have the luxury of looking at, working with, and thinking about Peter's work over months and years was a pleasure indeed.

I am first and foremost grateful to Peter for being a partner in every aspect of this venture, from the deepest intellectual issues to the smallest organizational details. His warmth, his undying good humor, and his generosity—both of spirit and of intellect—have made working with him truly a delight. He generously spent many hours with me in his studio discussing the work, questioning and challenging my thoughts and statements, which added immeasurably to the publication and to the exhibition. I am grateful for both his intellectual stimulation and his personal friendship.

Of course, no project of this scope can be accomplished by the curator and artist alone. I would in particular like to thank Peter Goulds and Kimberly Davis of L.A. Louver for their unflagging support and assistance along with that of current and former gallery staff including Gianna Carotenuto, Courtney Crane, Robin Ficara, and Jane Hart as well as Claire Roderick Keerl, Larry Levine, and Morgan Spangle (formerly at Louver Gallery, New York).

I would also like to acknowledge the generous financial support of numerous patrons and friends of the museum and of Peter Shelton: Alice and Nahum Lainer, Robert and Mary Looker, Jack and Bonnie Wilke, Marshall and Doris Redman, Merry Norris, Vivi-Ann and Harold Blankstein, Cliff and Mandy Einstein, Stanley and Elyse Grinstein, Anne and Bill Harmsen, Dallas and David Price, Darlene D. Sumner and Sumner Transport Corporation, and Dr. Beatrice Cooper. Their generosity, along with that of the National Endowment for the Arts, was crucial in bringing this exhibition to fruition. I am particularly indebted to Merry Norris for her assistance in securing support for the exhibition.

Numerous colleagues within the museum made important contributions to the exhibition. I am grateful for the encouragement of former directors Earl A. Powell III and Michael E. Shapiro as well as the assistance of Tom Jacobson of the museum's development department in securing funding. Elizabeth Algermissen and John Passi of the exhibitions department skillfully navigated various organizational shoals. Registrar Renée Montgomery and assistant registrar Tom Sacco carefully coordinated shipping arrangements. Arthur Owens, with his usual good humor, oversaw installation of the exhibition that was sensitively designed by Bernard Kester. Editor-in-chief Mitch Tuchman supervised the editing and production of the exhibition catalogue with acumen. Miyoshi Barosh carefully edited the catalogue, which was designed with flair by Scott Taylor. Photographer Jay K. McNally is responsible for the high quality of the catalogue's reproductions. Special thanks are due to Roz Leader, volunteer *par excellence* in the department of twentieth-century art, for her invaluable assistance both on the catalogue and on fund-raising.

Many other colleagues and friends provided advice, encouragement, and assistance in organizing this exhibition and catalogue. Thanks are due to Patty and Mark Anderson, Todd Anderson, Jacquelynn Baas, Darrell Benedict, Emily Braun, Diane Bromberg, Dick Bunker, Carol Caldwell, Gary Chew, Carl Davis, E. V. Day, Joe Diaz, Tim and Ginger Doyle, Rhona Edelbaum, Mercedes Elias, Thess Fennel, Tyler Fouts, Tom Freeberg, Richard Graham, Dr. Richard Hack, Don Harger, Dane Holweger, Sarah Hurlbert, E. J. Jarboe, Paul Johnson, Bayat Keerl, Sean Kelly, Kevin Komatsu, David Larson, Sandy Lunares, Gerald McGinnis and Fabrication Specialties, Ltd., Judy McInturff, Matt Magee, Clark Man, John Marshall, Mike Mironov, Dr. Ernest Nagamatsu, Ron Nolte, Paul Oliver, Dave Oltman, Alan Osborne, Chris Pate, Byron Peterson, Hayes Philo, Rutherford Poats and Lea Sneider, Chris Ponce, Robert Pyzocha, George Robinson, Brad Rude, Kurt Rude, Dale Ruffolo, Kay Scott, Steve Shackleford, David and Mary Shelton, Sharon Takeda, Walter Woods, and Colin Zaug.

Finally Peter Shelton and I would like to thank the lenders who kindly parted temporarily with significant works from their collections; without their generosity the museum could not have presented the breadth of Shelton's work as seen in this exhibition.

Carol S. Eliel

Associate curator, twentieth-century art

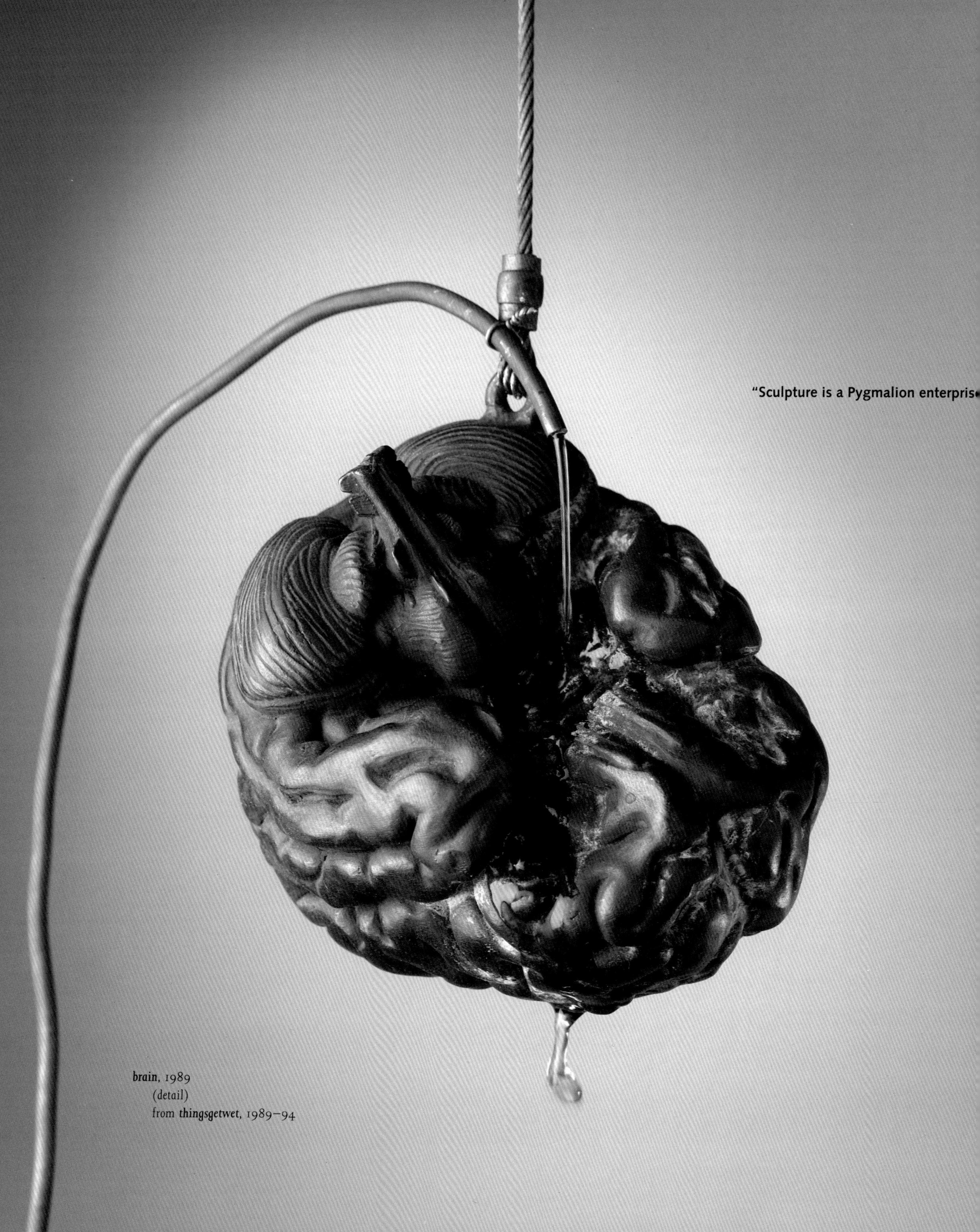

"Sculpture is a Pygmalion enterpris

brain, 1989
(detail)
from thingsgetwet, 1989–94

Carol S. Eliel

AN ARMATURE FOR OUR DESIRES

n which you are constantly trying to bring the dead to life."[1]

This exhibition of Peter Shelton's work is comprised of two components: a group of sculptures collectively known as **thingsgetwet**[2] and a selection of recent studio works, all made between 1986 and 1994. As varied as these works may seem, when seen in the context of Shelton's career they become part of a coherent whole. A combination of accessibility and mystery, an exploration of abstracted as well as figurative forms, an interest in architectural as well as anatomical motifs, a fascination with water, a tendency to layer forms (often ironically, counter to normal expectations), and various other recurring themes typical of Shelton's work are discussed in this essay.

Figure 1
Mockup of **thingsgetwet** in the interior courtyard of the Hood Museum, Dartmouth College, Hanover, New Hampshire, 1988

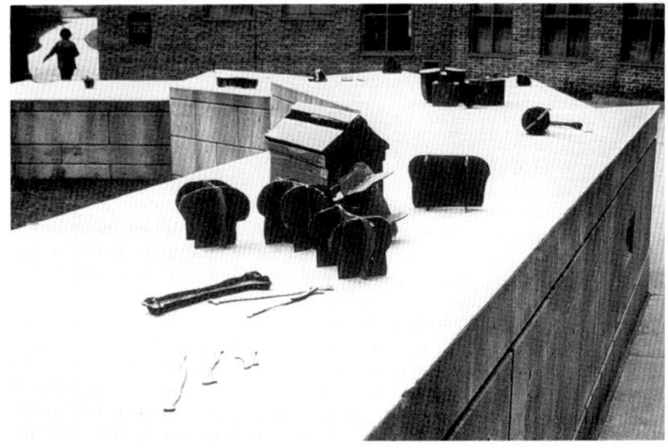

thingsgetwet was originally conceived as a commission for the interior courtyard of the Hood Museum at Dartmouth College, an institution that houses collections of art as well as of anthropological and ethnographic material.[3] The stepped courtyard suggested the original plan for the piece (fig. 1), which called for a series of relatively small, cast bronze objects to be positioned along the stepped concrete balustrade and bathed in water, which flowed from the top of the balustrade down to a catch basin at the bottom. The bronzes

1 Peter Shelton, including excerpts from an interview with Helaine Posner, 12 November 1985, *floatinghouse DEADMAN*, exh. cat. (Los Angeles: Wight Art Gallery, University of California, 1987), p. 7; hereafter, Shelton.

2 Shelton frequently titles his sculptures using all lowercase letters or unusual combinations of upper- and lowercase. According to the artist, he generally does this intuitively rather than for any specific reason.

3 Shelton feels that because of the anthropological nature of his art he was considered a particularly appropriate artist for this commission.

were, for the most part, representational depictions of such objects as a loaf of bread, bones and other anatomical parts, a house, a pair of boots, and a newborn baby, relating to the history of the institution as both an art and an anthropological museum. Shelton has referred to these objects as organs and the water as their life juice, a nonobjective and connective or mediating element. When the Dartmouth commission fell through and the possibility of exhibiting **thingsgetwet** at the Los Angeles County Museum of Art emerged, the bronze elements became over time more individuated and gradually transformed into the numerous independent sculptures of the large installation entitled **thingsgetwet** as it exists today.

Shelton has described **thingsgetwet** as

> *a collection of numerous small objects made of cast bronze collected in containers, hung from the ceiling, or arrayed variously on tables, shelves, chairs, beds, cabinets, and other structures of support. Each object is lightly bathed in water that runs in a self-contained capillary network of small tubes. The sources of these objects are diverse: zoological and medical, archaeo-logical and anthropological, architectural and sculptural, cultural and personal. The range of objects is as vast as the water is simple in its ability to mediate and soften these hard and varied things.*[4]

The objects depicted in **thingsgetwet** are all clearly recognizable though not necessarily immediately intelligible either individually or as a group. Each cast bronze element is laced with a network of thin copper pipes, through which a slow but steady stream of water is circulated by small electric pumps at the rate of approximately one quart per minute. The leitmotifs of Shelton's work repeat throughout the installation.

The themes of Shelton's work similarly repeat in the studio works that are shown here in conjunction with **thingsgetwet**. Sculptures such as **snakearm** (figs. 2–3), **blackdress** (fig. 4), and **fourleg** deftly toe the line between figuration and abstraction, between an interest in sculptural materials and an interest in organic form, and between a love of the

---

4 Shelton, unpublished notes, 1990.

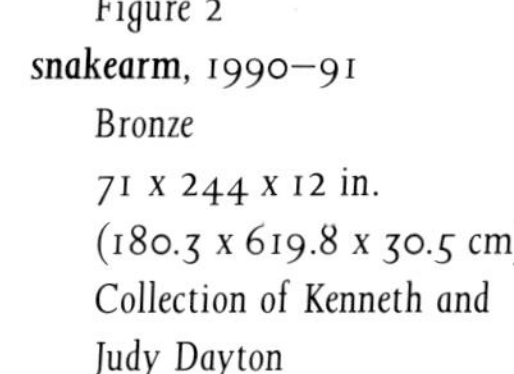

Figure 2
snakearm, 1990–91
Bronze
71 x 244 x 12 in.
(180.3 x 619.8 x 30.5 cm)
Collection of Kenneth and
Judy Dayton

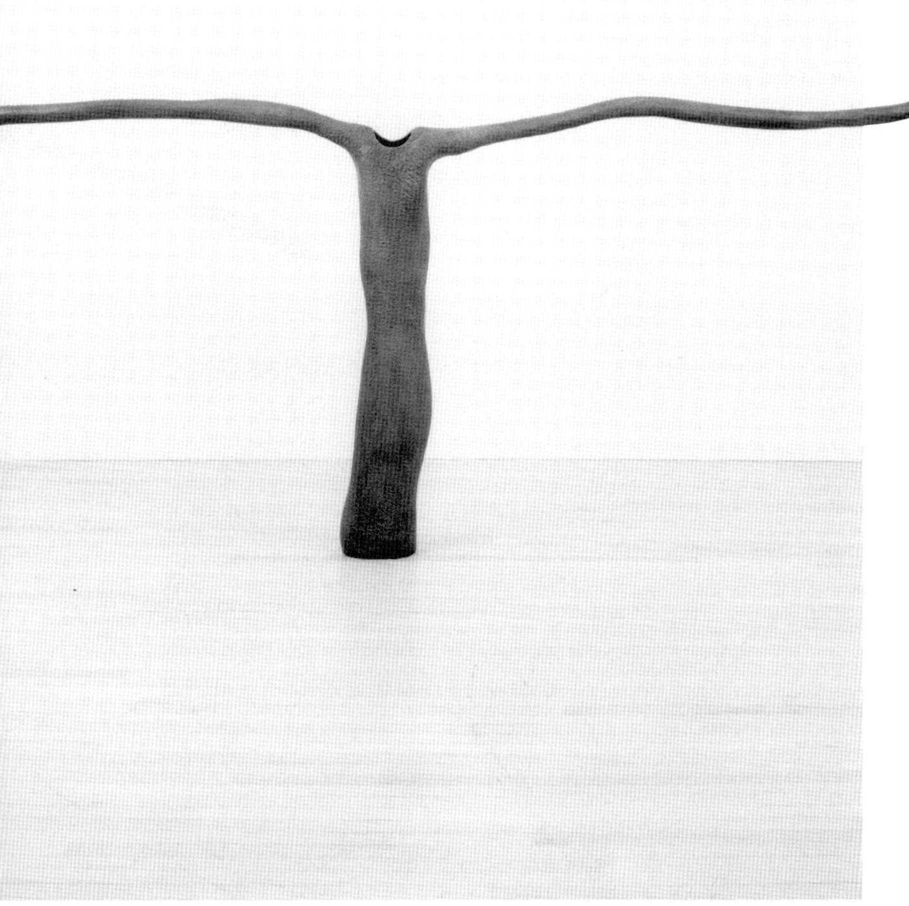

Figure 3
snakearm, 1990–91
(detail)

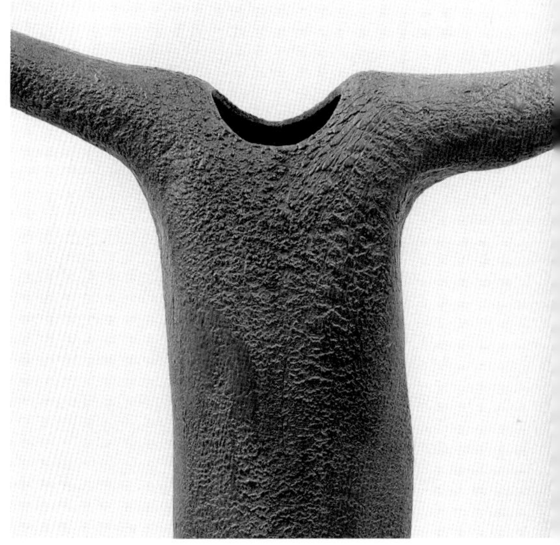

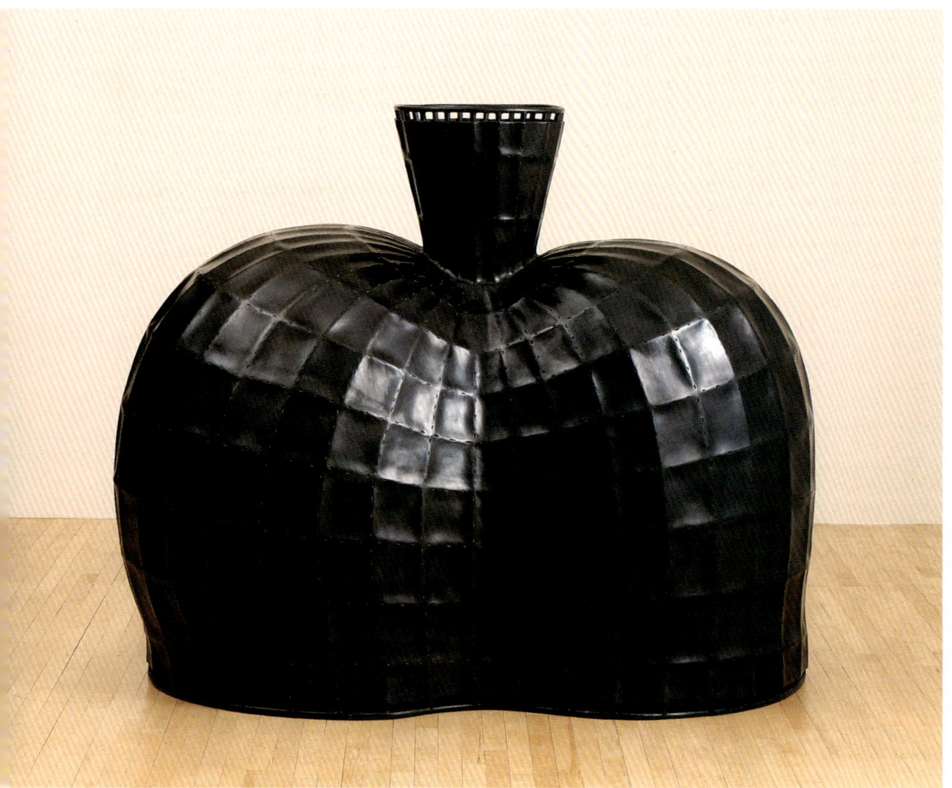

Figure 4
blackdress, 1990–91
Bronze
62 x 77 x 55 in.
(157.5 x 195.6 x 139.7 cm)
Private collection

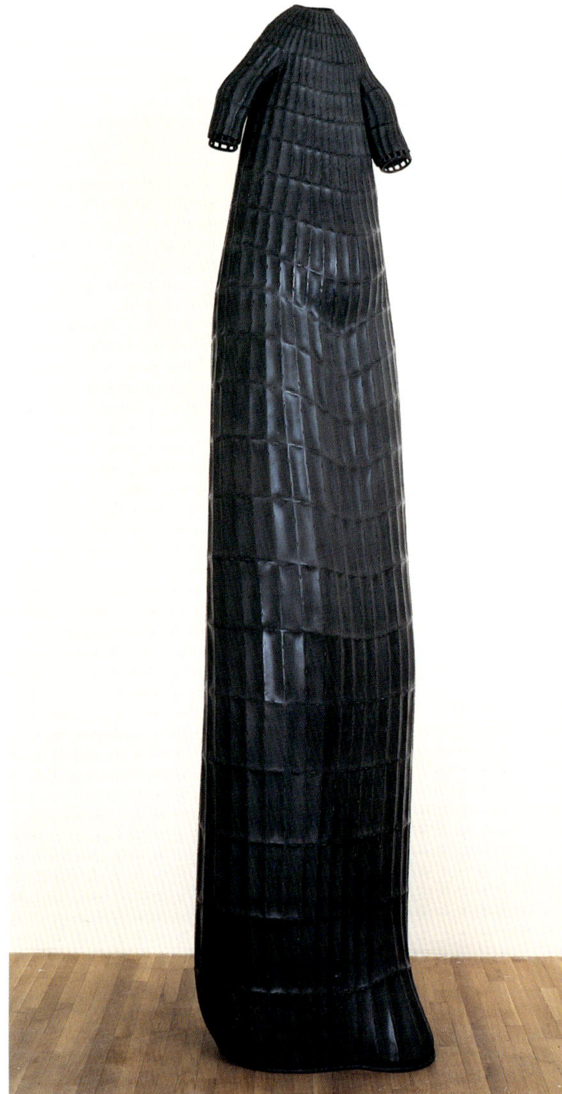

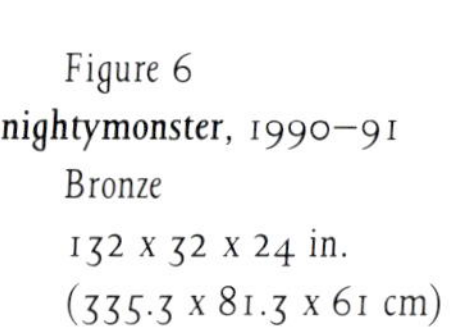

Figure 6
nightymonster, 1990–91
Bronze
132 x 32 x 24 in.
(335.3 x 81.3 x 61 cm)

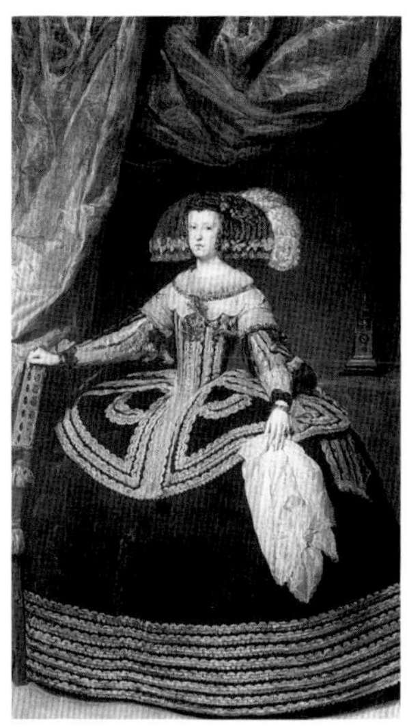

Figure 5
Diego *Velázquez*
Queen Mariana, c. 1652
Oil on canvas
91 x 51 5/8 in. (231 x 131 cm)
Museo del Prado, Madrid

human figure and a love of form for its own sake. **snakearm** conflates the human and the vegetal, as torso becomes tree trunk and human limbs become tree limbs. **blackdress**—inspired by Diego Velázquez's seventeenth-century portrait of Spain's Queen Mariana (fig. 5)—is at once a weighty, quasi-architectural presence with a hard metallic surface and a voluptuous, if abstracted, representation of a full female figure. The bulbous, rounded form of the Queen's skirt attached to the shaftlike form of her corseted chest suggests a Duchamp-like penetrated sexual object, be it bosom or buttocks. The stiff, horizontal bulk of **blackdress** is translated into a fluid, vertical presence in **nightymonster** (fig. 6), with its swelling belly and extremely long skirt. The comforting connotations of the word *nighty* and the maternal overtones implied by the pregnant figure contrast with the fearsome, looming, black metallic presence of the sculpture. While the grid pattern in **blackdress** seems merely to suggest a pattern in the fabric, here it resembles chain mail, weighing heavily on the outsized figure. An imagined monster of the night is, of course, a nightmare. Shelton has long been interested in dreams and has created characters that could inhabit just such a dream world.

Animated yet inert, referential yet abstracted, robust yet ethereal, easily read yet mysterious: Shelton's sculptures are filled with contradictions that infuse the work with many levels of interest: visual, physical, and psychological. This richness precludes Shelton's work from being categorized in terms of any one movement or "ism," be it postminimalism, postmodernism, conceptual art, or anything else. Instead, Shelton's is a body of work that demands to be considered on its own terms, considered both historically and ahistorically, both in the context of and outside Western art and culture.

Born in 1951 in Troy, Ohio, Shelton moved three years later to Tempe, Arizona, where he graduated from high school in 1969. In 1973 he received his bachelor's degree from Pomona College in Claremont, California, with a major in art (having, in turn, pursued majors in premedical studies, sociology, anthropology, and finally theater before turning to fine arts, which had been an interest of his since childhood). Although for practical reasons a painting major, Shelton's main interests already lay in the sculptural arena, including theater set design, which suggests the early importance for Shelton of movement in space and of the body's relationship to the space around it.

> *I was interested in theater because it had a bigger feel and a more complex form. From childhood I was always interested in creating environments which surrounded me. Painting, sculpture, and architecture as separate enterprises seemed entirely too specialized. The mixture of these things intrigued me. On some primal level I feel a natural continuum between these media as different manifestations of our adaptive and reflective needs to extend our bodies and psyches without us. In theater, when all its contemporary elaborations and complications are stripped away, a particular space [doesn't] need to have an actor, a simple viewer is sufficient. This situation could have some "literature" and defined space and movement associated with it, but it need not be that complicated or formalized. The literature could be very open-ended, revolving around the memories and allusions...of this viewer. And not everybody had to have the same literature going on at the same time either.*[5]

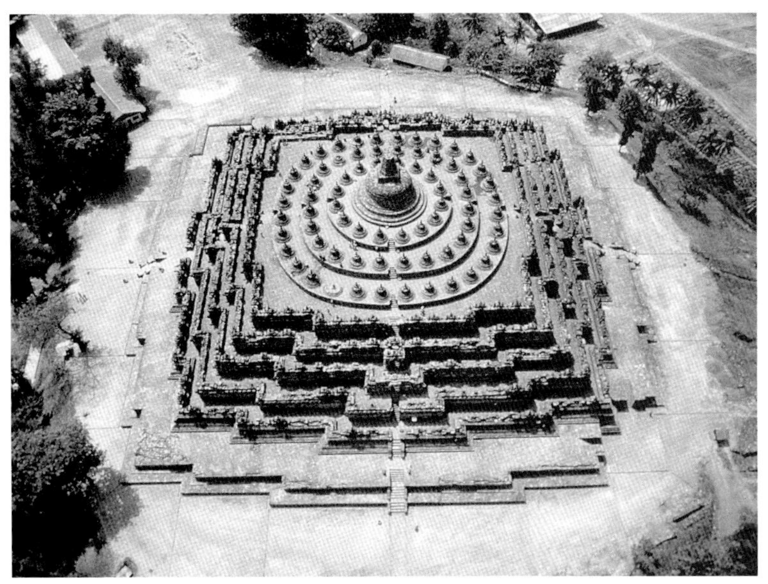

Figure 7
Borobudur, Java, Indonesia, late eighth century

As a student, Shelton was already interested in the creation of a total environment that would trigger the viewer's memories. The existence of this open-ended narrative element is critical for Shelton, as it allows the viewer to interact with the space not only physically or formally but also psychologically. In other words, the viewer experiences the space on a number of levels.

Shelton has repeatedly referred to the great, eighth-century Buddhist monument Borobudur (fig. 7) as the epitome of this combination of the physical and the psychological.

A series of stepped terraces (square at the bottom, circular at the top) creating a massive "temple-mountain" with a fixed itinerary of circumambulation, Borobudur "represents a Buddhist transition from the lowest manifestations of reality at the base, up through a series of 'regions' or psychological states, towards the ultimate condition of spiritual enlightenment and release from corruption and error at the summit."[6] A Buddhist pilgrim's total experience of Borobudur thus encompasses the physical experience of walking around and up the layered terraces, the intellectual experience of reading the Buddhist teachings from the monument's series of relief sculptures, and the aesthetic and spiritual experiences that emerge as a result. No environment of this sort can have a "right" or a "wrong" reading since the very act of arriving at an understanding of the meaning (or, perhaps more accurately, the meanings) of Borobudur is experiential. Shelton similarly expects his own sculptures to function both formally and in terms of content and to have within their narratives a structure encompassing the specific as well as the universal. His works do not have unique "right" readings but are open to various interpretations that are generated by the individual viewer.

In addition to its combination of experiences, Shelton has long been attracted to what he calls

> *that odd indecipherable quality [of Borobudur] between its being sculpture and its being architecture—something that interests me in my own work....From a certain distance, point of view, or stance, an object can be regarded as an object that is without, whole and definable; and then, with only a slight shift, we think of it as architecture, surrounding and open, something that you move around or into....The object is turned inside out, even dissolved. Our conventional Western boundary between sculpture as object (read figure) and architecture as space (read container-of-figure) becomes simplistic if not arbitrary in this context, especially when movement, time, and text (minimally, a thought) are introduced.*

This impulse to conflate the architectural and the sculptural is something that recurs throughout Shelton's body of work.

5 Shelton, interview with the author, 22 June 1993. In this essay all quotes from the artist, unless cited otherwise, are from interviews with the author on 14 May and 22 June 1993.

6 Philip Rawson, *The Art of Southeast Asia* (London: Thames and Hudson, 1967), p. 228.

After graduation from Pomona in 1973 Shelton returned to Troy, where he attended an eight-month trade course at the Hobart Brothers School of Welding Technology. Typically Shelton had a variety of reasons for doing this. For one, during the late 1960s and early 70s there was an emphasis on making an academic education relevant to the world outside the ivory tower. In addition, a number of his undergraduate teachers had recommended *against* his going to graduate school, which they perceived as overly academic and unnecessary to a career as an artist. Shelton also liked the idea of learning a trade that could allow him financial independence; and the idea of being back in Troy appealed to him as a way of discovering his midwestern roots (his earliest ancestors in this country were German blacksmiths who immigrated to Ohio in the late eighteenth century). Shelton has described this interlude in his life as "a bit innocent, but good and heroic, and I did have fantasies about retracing the footsteps of David Smith."[7]

Subsequent to completing trade certification at Hobart Brothers, Shelton worked as a welder in Ohio and then Michigan before returning to Los Angeles in late 1974. Determined to pursue a career as an artist, he chose to move to Los Angeles rather than to New York City; he had the impression that

> *L.A. was much more supportive because I would see "hybrid" artists like a Kienholz or a Nauman or Turrell or various people [who] were doing work out here [in Los Angeles] that always seemed more diverse, complete, and naturally polymorphous and much less ideological [than in New York]. This made their work ambitious and modest at once. Their work seemed to be more experiential and perceptually generated. Any "text" accumulated in these works came as much from the mind as from the body; the impact was more systemic than cerebral. This hit home.*[8]

Leaving painting behind him permanently, Shelton in his early years in Los Angeles focused on the dream books he had been keeping since his postgraduate sojourn in Ohio. These books were filled with images related to his dreams and fantasies. Without being illustrations, these were images that

7 Like Shelton, David Smith was born in the Midwest (Indiana) and worked for a summer at the Studebaker automobile factory before embarking on his career as an artist, first in New York City and subsequently in upstate New York. (Shelton's ancestry traces to the same Studebaker family.) Smith's first experiments with welded sculpture date to 1932–33, leading to masterpieces with autobiographical overtones such as *Home of the Welder*. Significantly for Shelton, Smith for many years worked simultaneously as a fine artist and as a machinist and welder.

8 Although the works of Ed Kienholz, Bruce Nauman, James Turrell, and other artists working in Los Angeles in the mid-1970s are stylistically and conceptually extremely varied, certain notions of what art is about—an interest in installation, in work that somehow relates to the body, and in work that is experienced both physically and conceptually—were commonly held by these artists as opposed to artists working in New York at that time. It was the prevalence of such aspects of art being made in Los Angeles that appealed to Shelton.

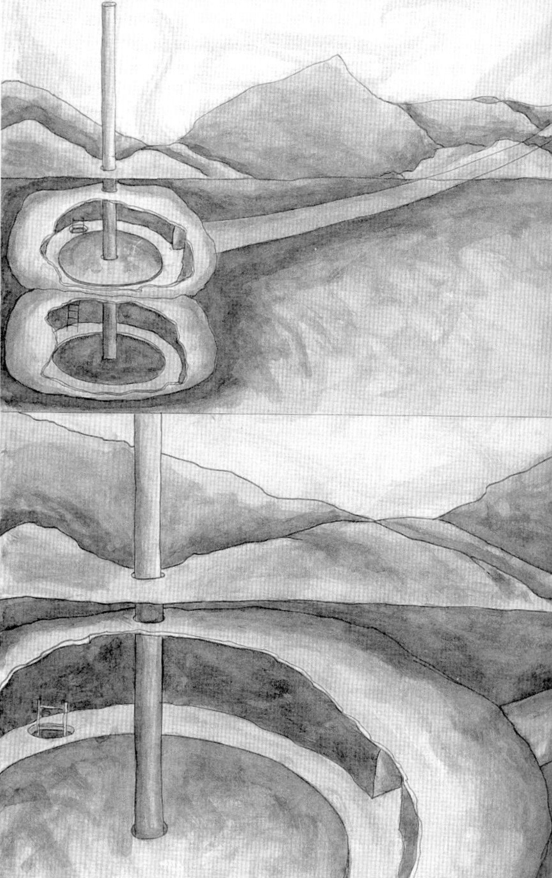

had a kind of integrity about them, like a tree growing out of the ground, and a quality of bigness that had a way of putting other things into perspective. What was appealing about them was they didn't feel so technical, formal, or self-conscious. Obviously, there was something easy about the attractiveness of images sometimes so fantastic, but at the same time...there was some real human basis, some fundamental relationship to my work.

These drawings emerged from the fantastic or intuitive aspects of Shelton's creative imagination yet were very much grounded in reality. Interestingly some of the earliest drawings were of tubes, pipes, simple vessel forms, and conduits—forms that Shelton early on perceived as "some kind of metabody, often thinking of the work as if it were an organism or an organ system." Shelton frequently made analogies between the formal structures of his sculptures and the human body and psyche. In his early drawings he was already interested in "layering, or archaeological stratification, as a compositional device: layers of space and layers of the body and layers of consciousness" (fig. 8). A purely formal or phenomenal approach to art was not enough to satisfy him. Art had to encompass imagery, memory, ideas, and responses (i.e., form, concept, and narrative) in order to be complete and to fulfill his—and by extension, the viewer's—needs.

Figure 8
Over and under, longtunnel, 1976
India ink and felt pen on cardboard
49 x 31 ½ in. (124.5 x 80 cm)
Collection of Sharon Takeda and Peter Shelton

By 1975 Shelton's ideas about the totality of the sculptural statement were already in place. "I don't see concept being at odds with the body," he has stated, "and I don't see form being at odds with concept. I never have, any more than I see my body being in conflict with my mind....We might want to choose at times, but polarity drives the motor of life. It seems to me that this [apparent] contradiction is the thing that sculpture is best at addressing." From the earliest drawings to the most recent work, Shelton has wrestled with various means to create and express the same ideas. The wide range of figuration and abstraction in his work points to the breadth of these various means, as does the constant presence or suggestion of the body as well as the layering of both forms and narrative.

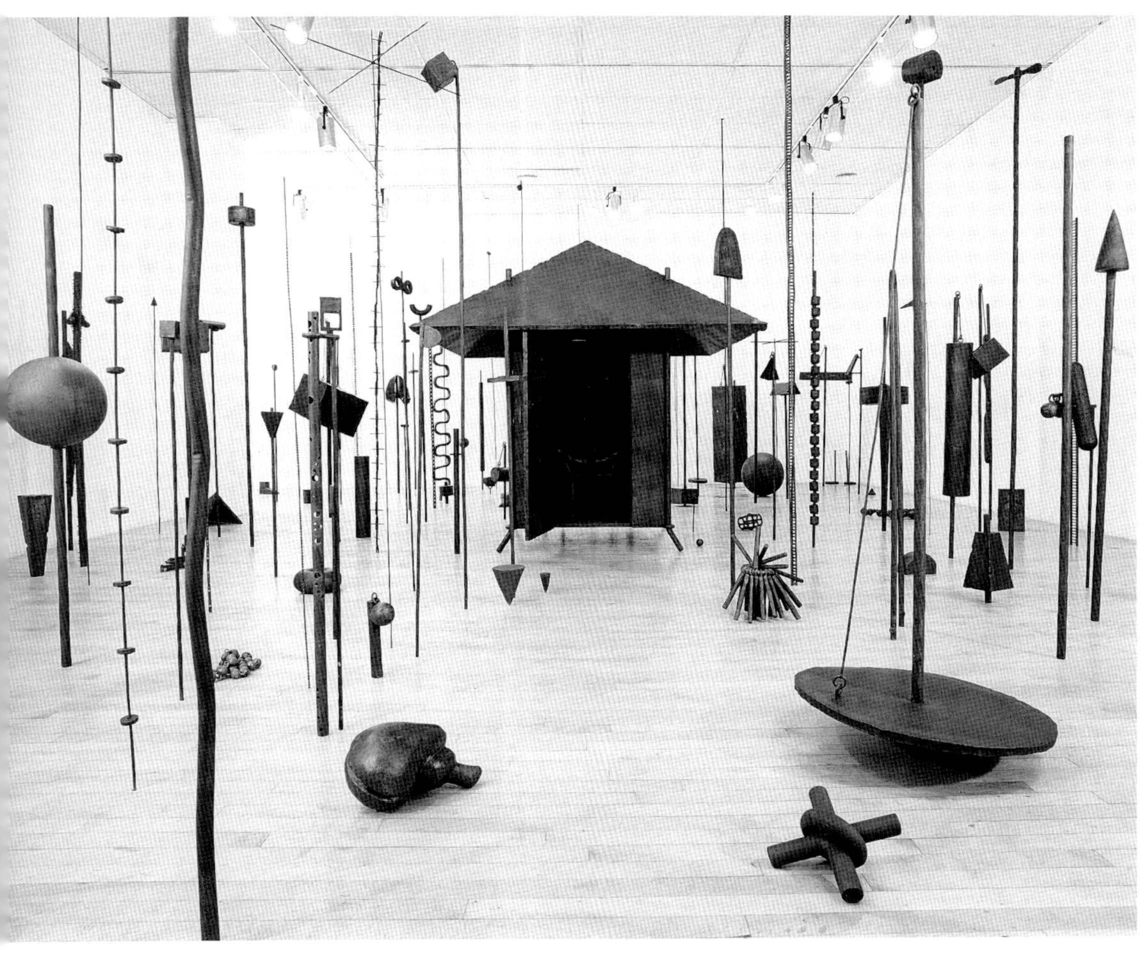

Figure 10
SWEATHOUSE and little principals
(150 elements), 1977–82
Steel
Dimensions variable
Installation view, Contemporary Arts Forum, Santa Barbara, California

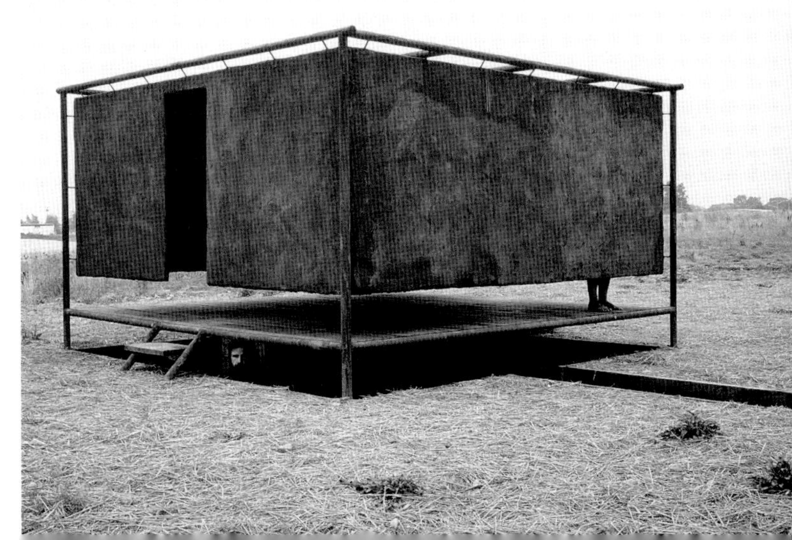

Figure 11
HEADROOM footspace, 1980
Steel, wood, and cement
14 x 26 x 12½ ft.
(4.3 x 7.9 x 3.8 m)
Installation view, Artpark, Lewiston, New York

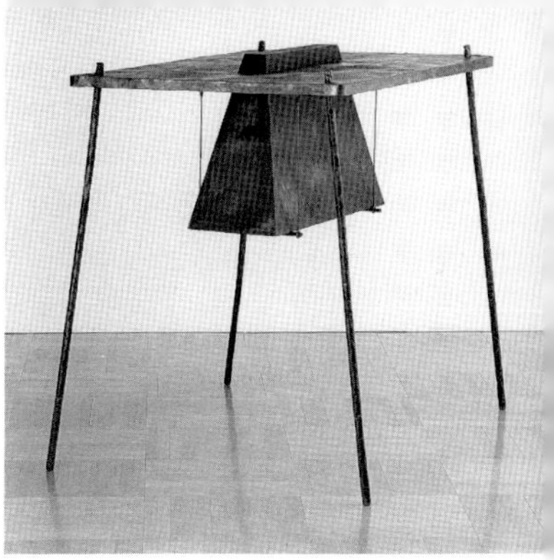

Between 1975 and 1977 Shelton used the facilities at Claremont Graduate School and the University of California, Los Angeles (UCLA), to make his sculptures. Works from the mid-70s, such as **trapeze** (fig. 9), play on a formalized anthropomorphism that make evident his concept of sculpture as "metabody," as a parallel to our own physical states.

He enrolled in graduate school at UCLA in 1977 and began working on **SWEATHOUSE and little principals** (fig. 10), which was originally exhibited in 1979 and later amplified for a 1982 installation. This was Shelton's first large-scale project to address the wide range of his concerns and realize his ambitions in three dimensions.[9] We see here an interest in architectural forms and in forms that reflect the human body as well as an interest in layering and cataloging forms in space, leitmotifs that run throughout Shelton's work. It is important to note that the **little principals** include both highly abstract forms as well as extremely graphic elements such as a brain or a loaf of bread. The installation stresses the polarity between the empty and mute **SWEATHOUSE** and the army of anthropomorphic **little principals** surrounding it. Shelton has spoken of the "buoyancy" of the **little principals**, suspended as many of them are on poles, and suggested that this "wasn't unlike seeing a collection of things floating in water." Shelton values the physical, spiritual, and dream associations of water, which began to play an ongoing role in his work as mediator, purifier, and buoying element.

Shelton's interest in the layering of both suspended and buried forms recurs in **HEADROOM footspace** (fig. 11), created in 1980 for Artpark in Lewiston, New York. An inversion of "normal" layering, both top to bottom and light to heavy, occurs here. After entering **HEADROOM**, the viewer finds his head at foot level to the rest of the world. Although most of his body is below ground, he is still able to look outside. By contrast, **footspace** hovers above, hiding the viewer's trunk, arms, and head, while his feet remain exposed to the outside world. The viewer, though above ground, cannot see out of the enclosed space surrounding him.

Figure 9
trapeze, 1977
Steel
64 x 48 x 72 in.
(162.6 x 121.9 x 182.9 cm)
Collection of Sharon Takeda and Peter Shelton

9 Shelton, p. 8.

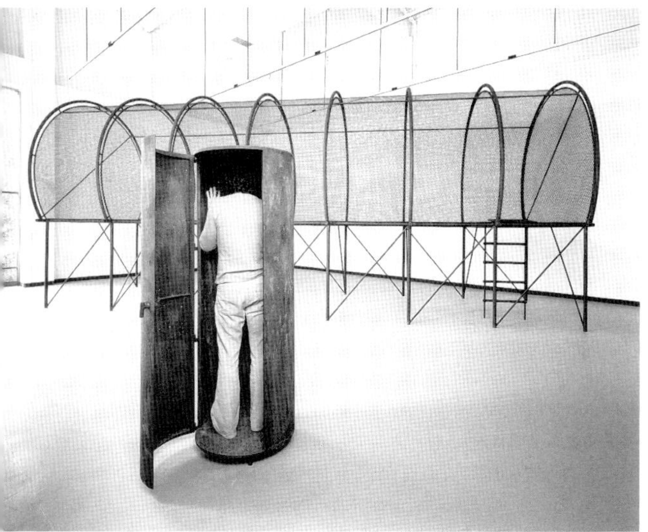

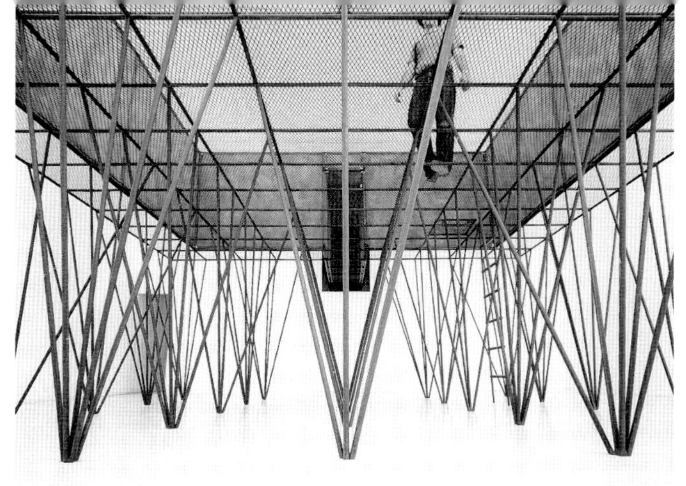

Figure 12
BIRDHOUSE **holecan**, 1980
BIRDHOUSE
Steel
13½ x 10½ x 28 ft.
(4.1 x 3.2 x 8.5 m)
holecan
Steel
72 x 25 in. (182.9 x 63.5 cm)
Installation view, Chapman College, Orange, California

Figure 13
NECKWALL **footscreen, sleeper**, 1980–81
Steel and cloth
12 x 17½ x 17½ ft.
(3.7 x 5.3 x 5.3 m)
Installation view, Malinda Wyatt Gallery, Venice, California

Figure 14
MAJORJOINTS **hangers and squat**, 1983
Steel, cast iron, and cement
Dimensions variable
Installation view, Malinda Wyatt Gallery, Venice, California

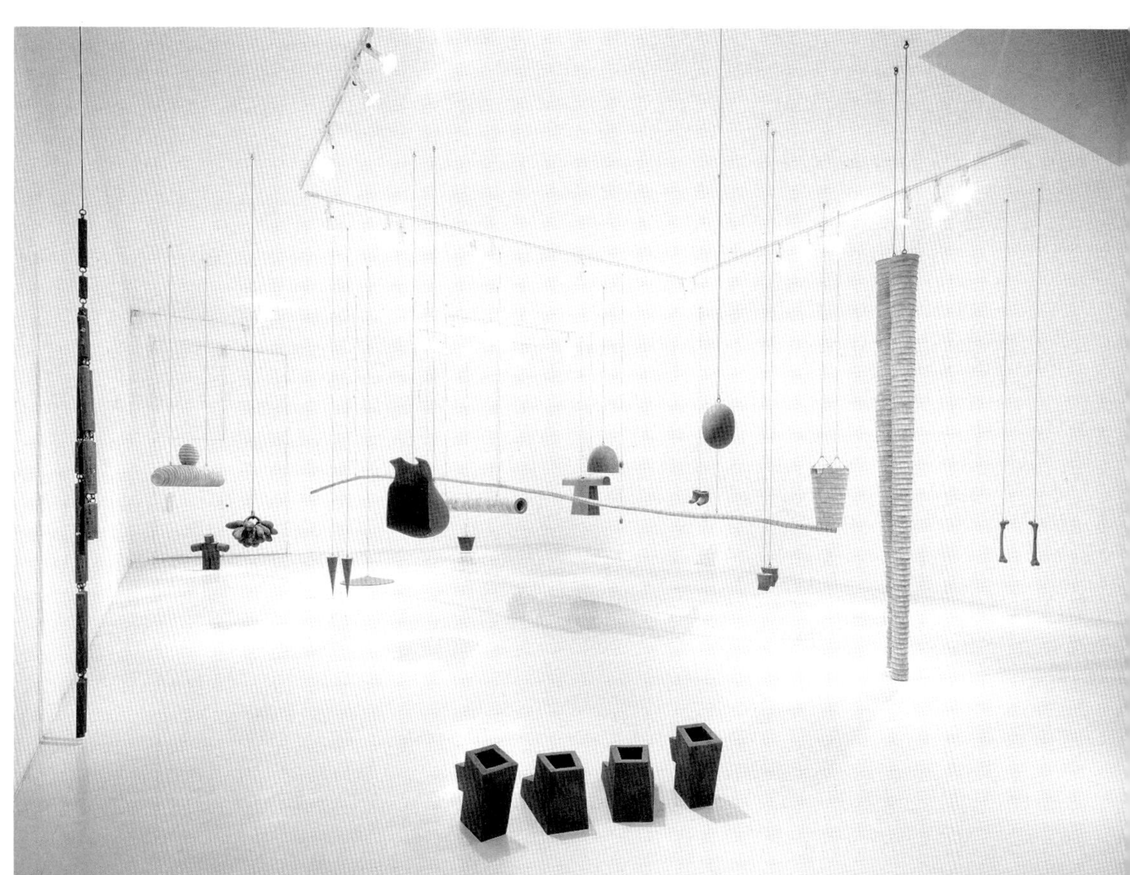

An analogous spatial contrast, again ironically inverted, is seen in **BIRDHOUSE holecan** (fig. 12) of the same year. **BIRDHOUSE** appears to be very open but is, in fact, cagelike, psychologically rather than physically trapping the viewer. By contrast, although **holecan** appears to be very claustrophobic and coffinlike, ample light and air enter through seven hundred small holes that map the bodies of twenty-five of Shelton's family members. Shelton's forms refer to skeleton and skin, further stressing the intimate relationship between his sculptures and the body.

This notion of a sculptural skin figuratively reflecting the living form is another theme that recurs in Shelton's sculptures. In a work such as **NECKWALL footscreen, sleeper**, 1980–81 (fig. 13), parchment-colored cloth covers the skeletal structure of the architecture "as if you were taking your skin off and stretching it onto a frame...a way of keeping that connection to the body." Once again, space in **NECKWALL footscreen, sleeper** is layered and topsy-turvy; the viewer's feet hover above eye level. Just as in **HEADROOM**, the viewer standing inside **NECKWALL** becomes an important part of the sculpture. The transparent and floating qualities of the floor of **NECKWALL**, are worth noting, not only as being related to dreams—also suggested by the bed reference in **sleeper**—but as an early reference to water.

The conflation of subject and object, of viewer and sculpture suggested in **NECKWALL** is made explicit in **MAJORJOINTS hangers and squat**, 1983 (figs. 14–15). References to the human torso, skull, calves, feet, and so forth are quite obvious, yet most of the forms range from the highly abstracted to the completely abstract. The conduit or pipe forms hark back to the early drawings and prefigure later works such as **clearcuttubesandpipes**. **MAJORJOINTS hangers and squat** was the first of Shelton's installations to be made up primarily of cast pieces. The metal elements of earlier works such as **SWEATHOUSE and little principals** were largely built up out of plate or sheet metal and tubing.

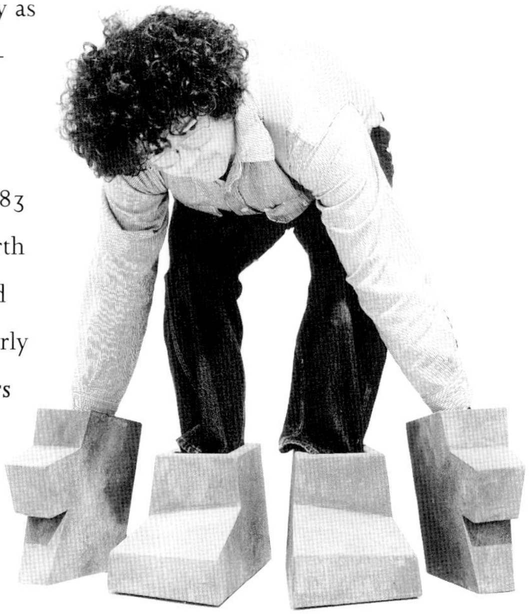

Figure 15
shoes and gloves, 1983
from **MAJORJOINTS hangers and squat** (with Peter Shelton)
Cast iron
Dimensions variable
Private collection

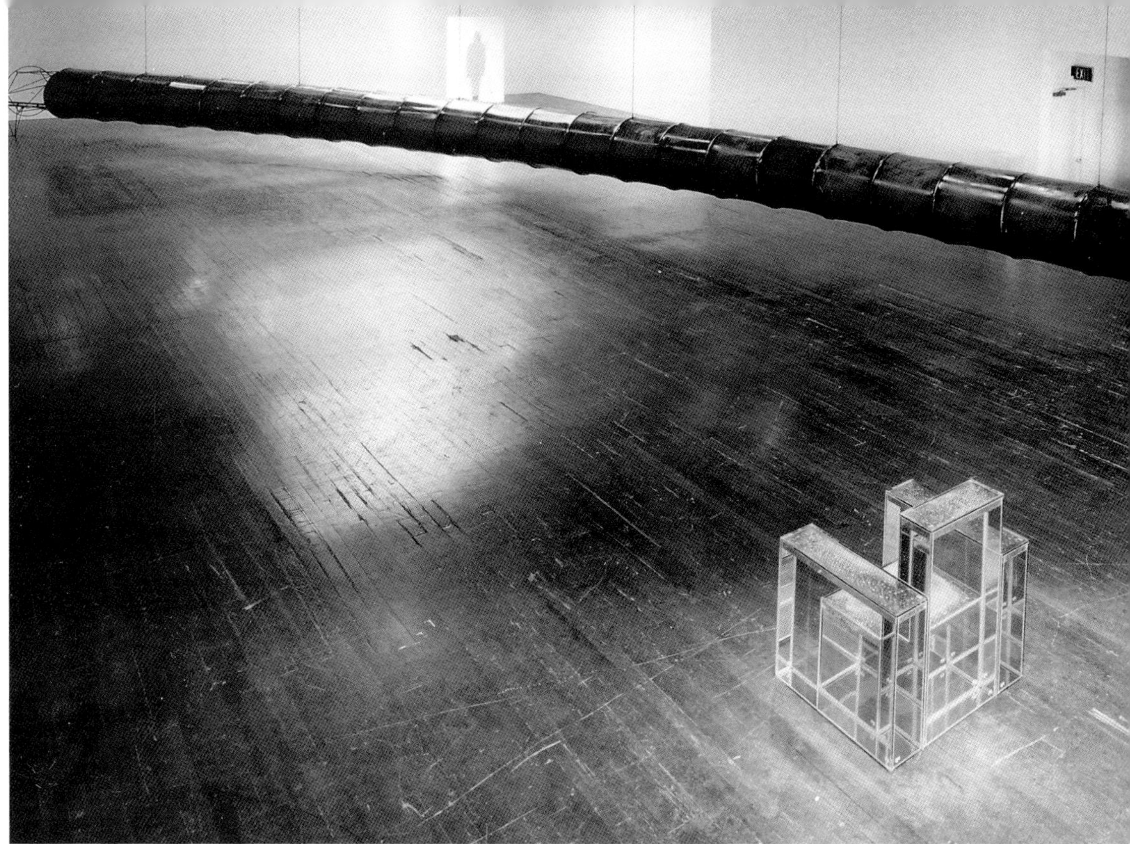

Specific references to pipes and water—and their relationship to the viewer—appear in **pipegut, waterseat and STANDSTILL**, 1983–84 (figs. 16–17). All three elements of this work are informed by the distinctions between real and projected experience and between body-as-sensor and body-as-object. Shelton has described the work succinctly:

> **pipegut** *is a gently curving, skinned-steel tensile structure—maybe an intestine or birth canal—hanging from the gallery ceiling. A track running through its interior conveys a small car upon which one may move pulling oneself hand over hand.* **waterseat** *is a waterfilled glass throne that is perhaps a bit amniotic and inviting but pristine and fragile as well. One feels coarse or heavy sitting on it.* **STANDSTILL** *is a cast concrete panel with a central "negative" just big enough to stand in. A visitor to the interior of this dead mass is rendered soft, transient, even delicate—like leaves in the gutter. The objective aspects of these works form strong contrasts to their experiential interiors. One has both the nut and the shell.*[10]

The three components of this installation can be seen as metaphors for birth, life, and death. Just as these anchor the human experience, reality for Shelton is formed out of the widely divergent elements epitomized by the individual components of **pipegut, waterseat and STANDSTILL**.

10 Shelton, p. 17.

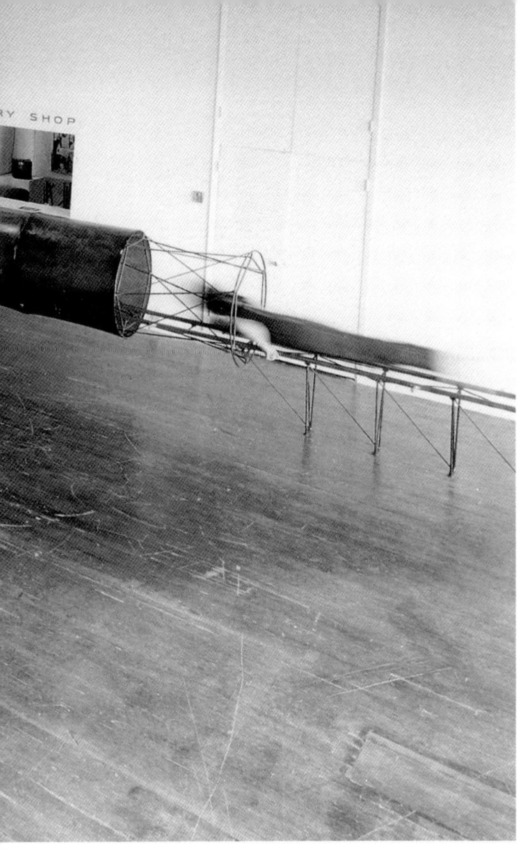

Figure 16
pipegut, waterseat and STANDSTILL, 1983–84
pipegut
Steel, cloth, and shellac
length: 96 ft. (29.3 m);
diameter: 40 in. (101.6 cm)
waterseat
Plate glass and water
40 x 36 x 32 in.
(101.6 x 91.4 x 81.3 cm)
STANDSTILL
Concrete
96 x 48 x 14 in.
(243.8 x 121.9 x 35.6 cm)
Installation view, Portland Center for the Visual Arts, Oregon

Figure 17
STANDSTILL and **pipegut**, 1983–84
from **pipegut, waterseat and** STANDSTILL

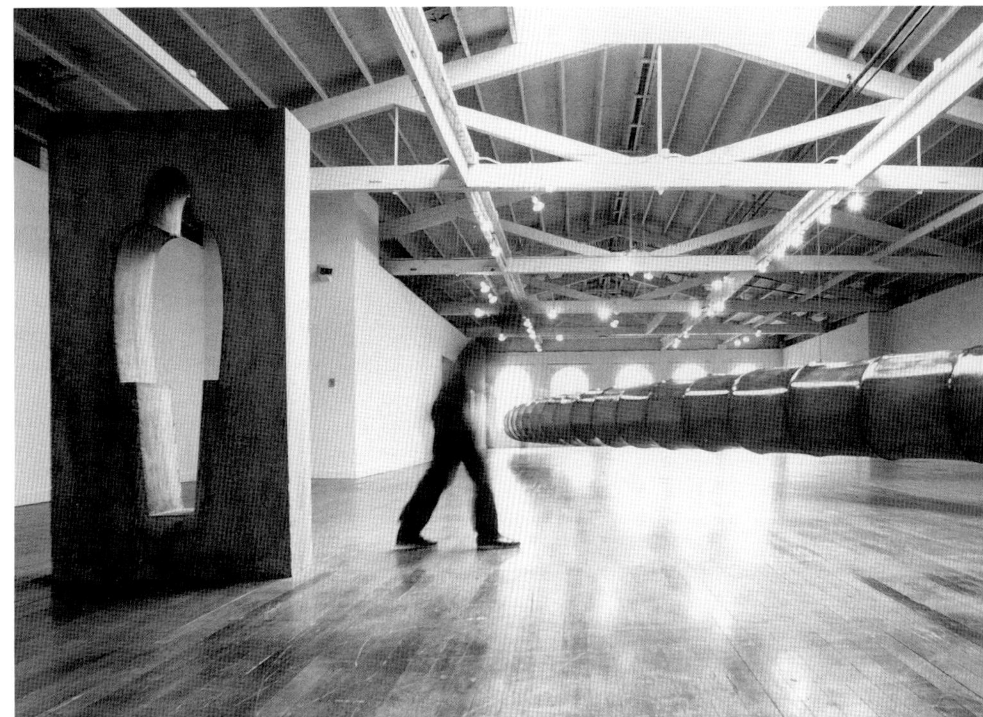

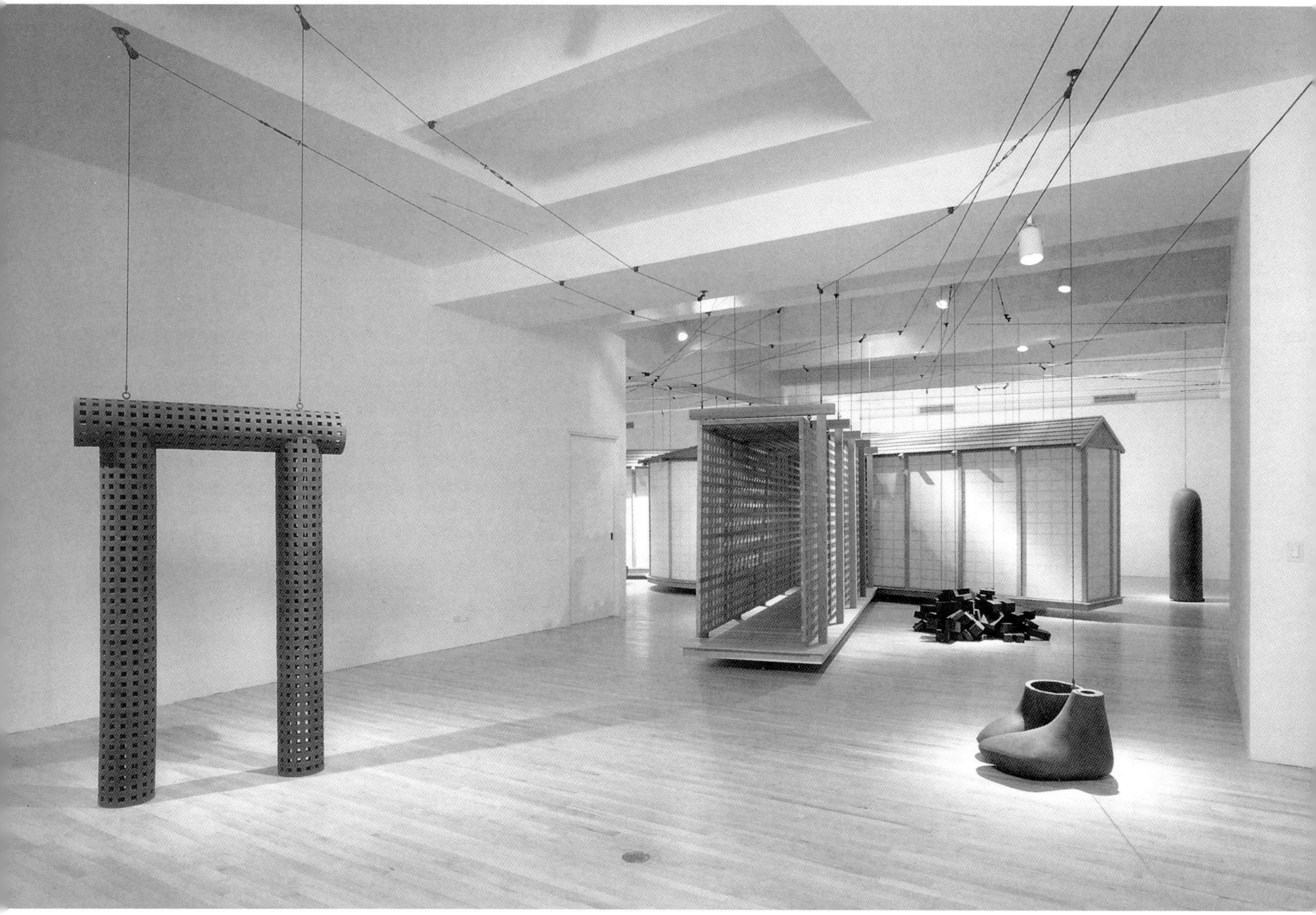

Figure 18
floatinghouseDEADMAN, 1985–86
Wood, paper, cast iron, steel, concrete, and water
Dimensions variable
Installation view, Louver Gallery, New York City

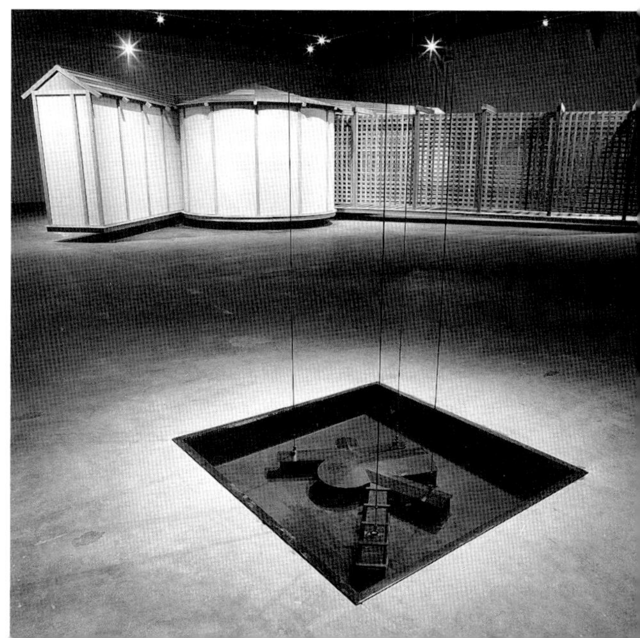

Figure 20
sunkenhouse, 1985
from **floatinghouse**DEADMAN, 1985–86
Cast iron, steel, and water
16 x 51 x 54 in.
(40.6 x 129.5 x 137.2 cm)
Installation view, Herron Gallery, Indianapolis Center for Contemporary Art

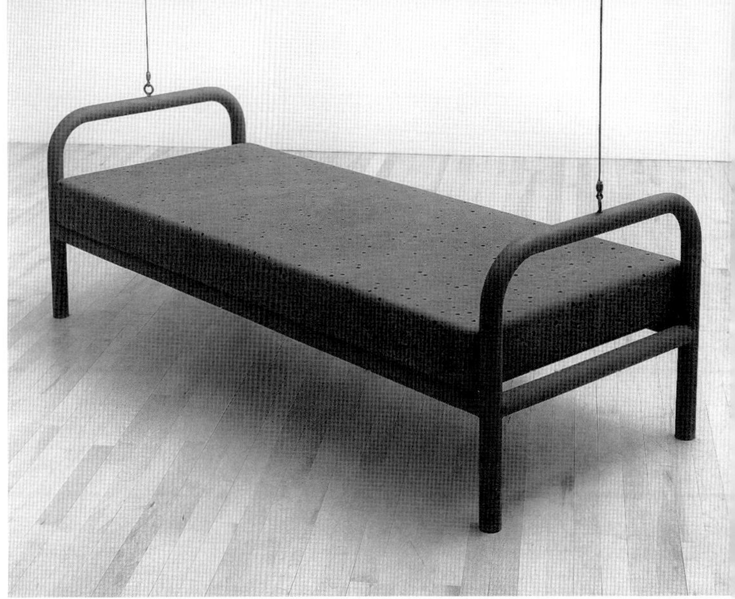

Figure 19
holebed, 1985
from **floatinghouseDEADMAN**, 1985–86
Steel
26 x 76 x 30 in.
(66 x 193 x 76.2 cm)
Installation view, Louver Gallery, New York City

floatinghouseDEADMAN (fig. 18) was originally created in 1985–86 for exhibition at the gallery of the University of Massachusetts at Amherst. The themes of Shelton's work reappear: the relation of the body to surrounding space, the conflation of sculpture and architecture, the conflation of sculpture and the human figure, the suggestion of a text or narrative, layering and reversed expectations, and an interest in the associations evoked by the use of water and suspended objects. **floatinghouse**, a large paper and wood structure clearly informed by Japanese architecture, hovers several inches off the floor. The "house" is attached by cables to a series of fourteen cast metal and concrete counterweights ("deadmen" in construction jargon) in a wide variety of forms, including: an abstracted, spread-eagled human figure (the *deadman* of the title); a skeleton; a bed (fig. 19); a seven-foot-tall mallet; large, abstracted feet; a chair; and even a small model of **floatinghouse**, titled **sunkenhouse** (fig. 20).

In Shelton's words, **floatinghouseDEADMAN**

> *depend[s] on reversals and contrasts. Things that are heavy should be down around your feet, but you could unexpectedly find them up around your ears. Concepts that are thought to have no physical weight can achieve major mass. Space that is thought to surround becomes a stone at your feet. What you think is inside is the outside of something else. A gigantic thing may become small at the right distance. Certainly a house cannot float?*[11]

floatinghouse itself is an anthropomorphic form, whose plan Shelton derived from the outlines of his own body, to which "a long one-end-rounded room was added as if [he] had swallowed a small nave and apse of a church."[12] The viewer can enter **floatinghouse**, a cedar-wood skeleton with a paper skin, through one limb and exit through another. This conflation of architecture, the human figure, and sculpture is more visually comprehensible in the smaller form of **sunkenhouse**, which also points to Shelton's recurrent and ironic reversals of expectations. **floatinghouse**, the large form made of paper and

11 Shelton, p. 7.

12 Ibid., p. 19.

wood, is hollow, light, and suspended in air. In contrast, the diminutive **sunkenhouse**, made of solid steel and iron, is heavy, dense, and literally submerged in water below floor level.

The juxtaposition of readily recognizable elements in **floatinghouseDEADMAN** suggests a specific narrative; however, as in all of Shelton's work, no such narrative exists. Rather, the work developed as an "accretion of technical, formal, fanciful, and imaginative responses to the given space." The range in **floatinghouseDEADMAN**—from heavy to light objects, from compact to elongated forms, from giant to diminutive scale—is as varied as the interpretations that can be brought to bear by its audience. At the same time these varied readings necessarily emerge from shared understandings based on basic human experience.

TUB, tubes and pipes of 1987 (fig. 21) again addresses the relationships between the human figure and space and between sculpture and architecture using the vessel and conduit forms seen in the early drawings. **TUB** is both an architectural form, a squat box with drains, and a figural form, a squat torso with short, stubby arms. **tubes and pipes** is comprised of Shelton's basic vocabulary of vessel and conduit forms with both biological references (e.g., limbs, intestines, blood vessels) and with hydraulic, pneumatic, and plumbing references. In **TUB** a torso becomes architecture; in **tubes and pipes** architectural elements evolve into organic forms. The contrasts between cast concrete and bronze, between hard, rectilinear and soft, organic forms, and between geometric containment and free-form spread are striking, as are the nascent and vestigial references to the human body in this sculptural installation.

BLACKVAULTfalloffstone, 1988 (fig. 22), reflects Shelton's ongoing fascination with inverted spaces, both top to bottom and inside to outside, as well as with sculpture as architecture and with the figure's relationship to space. **BLACKVAULT** is a massive, heavy form, cast of black concrete in a pit, which was then laboriously excavated, turned upside down, and mounted on ten relatively thin, metal "legs." The sculpture literally becomes

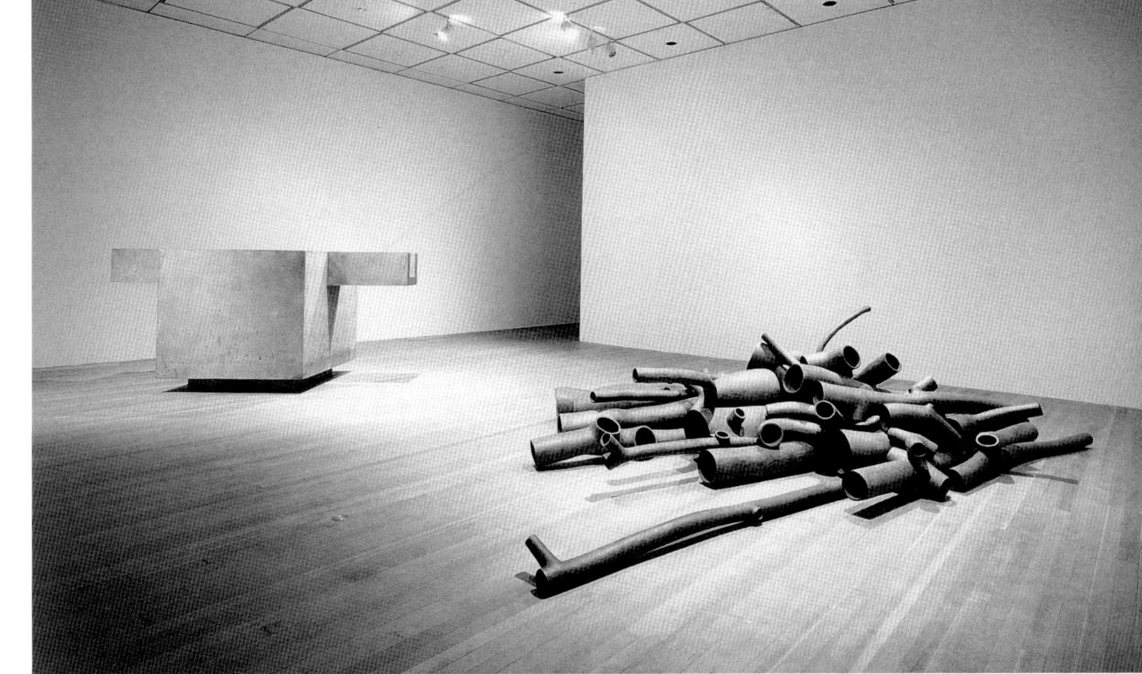

Figure 21
TUB, tubes and pipes, 1987
TUB
Concrete
60 x 132 x 60 in.
(150 x 340 x 150 cm)
tubes and pipes
Bronze
48 x 192 x 144 in.
(120 x 490 x 370 cm)
Installation view, University of California, Irvine

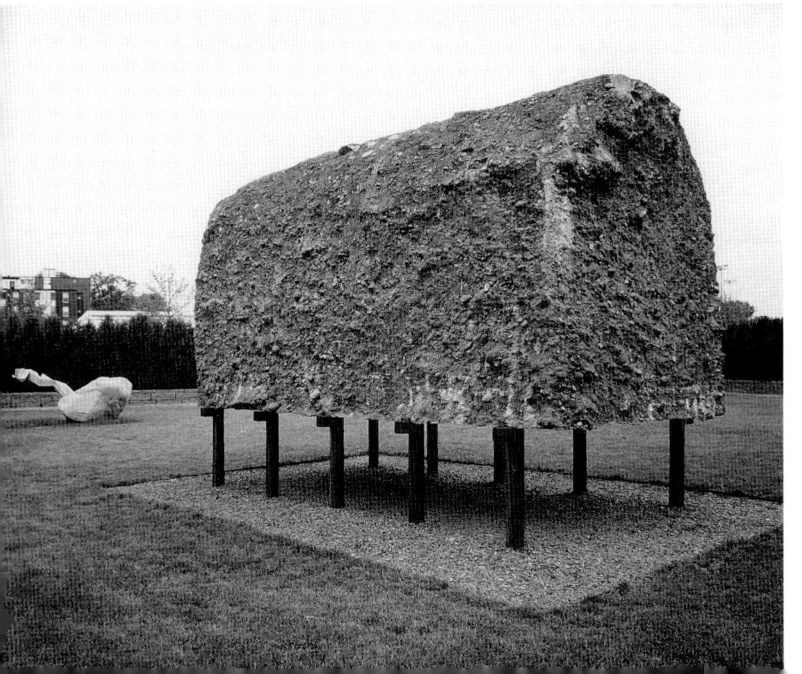

Figure 22
BLACKVAULT**falloffstone**, 1988
BLACKVAULT
Concrete and steel
142 x 105 x 197 in.
(360.7 x 266.7 x 500.4 cm)
falloffstone
Stone and aluminum
53 x 67 x 116 in.
(134.6 x 170.2 x 294.6 cm)
Installation view, Walker Art Center, Minneapolis

an architectural form (or perhaps vice-versa), a fact emphasized by its title. **BLACKVAULT** is a room that isolates the viewer in the same way **footspace** does. Once inside the vaulted space the viewer's head and torso are hidden, and only his feet and legs are visible to the outside world. Not only has the form itself been inverted from its casting position to its position overhead, but the notion of a cast form and its inside surface has also been everted here. The exterior is rough, revealing the process by which it was made, while the interior is smooth and highly finished.

Just as in earlier works the nonobjective form of **BLACKVAULT** contrasts with the figural form of **falloffstone**. The closed-to-the-sky, weighty bulk of **BLACKVAULT** contrasts with the open-to-the-sky, airborne quality of **falloffstone**. The viewer can lie in the figural shell component of **falloffstone**, thereby becoming part of the sculpture. Because of the cantilevered position of this figural element, it is impossible for a viewer lying in it to determine his position vis-à-vis the ground. Although the body's relationship to space is the defining element of **falloffstone**, it is ironically incomprehensible to that body.

The numerous elements of **thingsgetwet** exist as independent sculptures, though they were conceived of collectively as a large-scale installation. Created between 1989 and 1994, they may superficially suggest a marked departure for Shelton, yet this body of work addresses the same issues and grapples with the same concerns that the artist has dealt with throughout his career. As in **floatinghouseDEADMAN**, the elements of **thingsgetwet** suggest the existence of an explanatory narrative, both individual and collective. Yet, as with the earlier work, no specific or given narrative exists. Instead we are faced with a collection of discrete objects whose "range is as vast as the water is simple in its ability to mediate and soften these hard and varied things."[13]

The water is a

way [of] reconciling the multitude of different things in life, a universal solvent. All of our different purposes as well as our biological and spiritual responses to things seem to be very compartmentalized, fragmented, and distributed into hierarchies. There's a brutality in this clarity. [The use of water] has

13 Shelton, unpublished notes, 1990.

both a healing and erosive or leveling effect on all these "perfect" things.... Our pride is dissolved.... [Water] is a sort of "ethereum," it's the nonobjective, it's the spatial that is in contrast to the objective, to the hard, to the separate. It is palpable yet abstract; bloody yet pure.

For Shelton the hanging of **floatinghouseDEADMAN** is intimately related to the bathing of **thingsgetwet**; both are similar means to challenge the materiality and certainty of the object. In fact, hanging his sculptures rather than placing them on the ground has long been a strategy of Shelton's. The idea of suspending sculptures from above was in part an extension of his desire to minimize the base and to maximize the presence and associations of the sculptures themselves. Suggestions of this can already be seen in early works such as **trapeze**, in which thin legs project the more substantial body of the sculpture into the air. The poles in **SWEATHOUSE and little principals** similarly make anthropomorphic references while simultaneously elevating larger sculptural forms to heights ranging from only a few inches off the floor to twelve feet in the air. Shelton frequently uses poles or legs as devices to lift his sculptures off the floor without resorting to the large and ungainly pedestals that would have been necessary to support many of his large and/or heavy sculptural elements. He has spoken of hanging sculptures "as a way of floating them," likening suspension in air to floating in water, as he did earlier in **NECKWALL**, in **floater** of 1982 (fig. 23), and in **floatinghouseDEADMAN**.

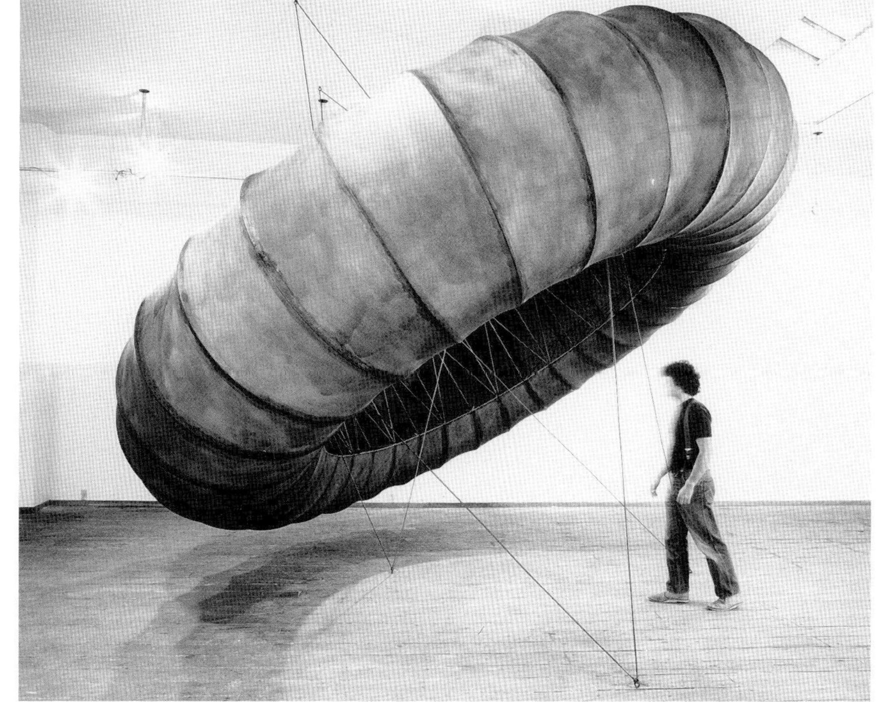

Figure 23
floater, 1982
from **trunknuts WHITEHEAD floater**
Steel and cloth
diameter: 18 ft. (5.5 m); cross section: 54 in. (137.2 cm)
Installation view, Open Space Gallery, Victoria, British Columbia

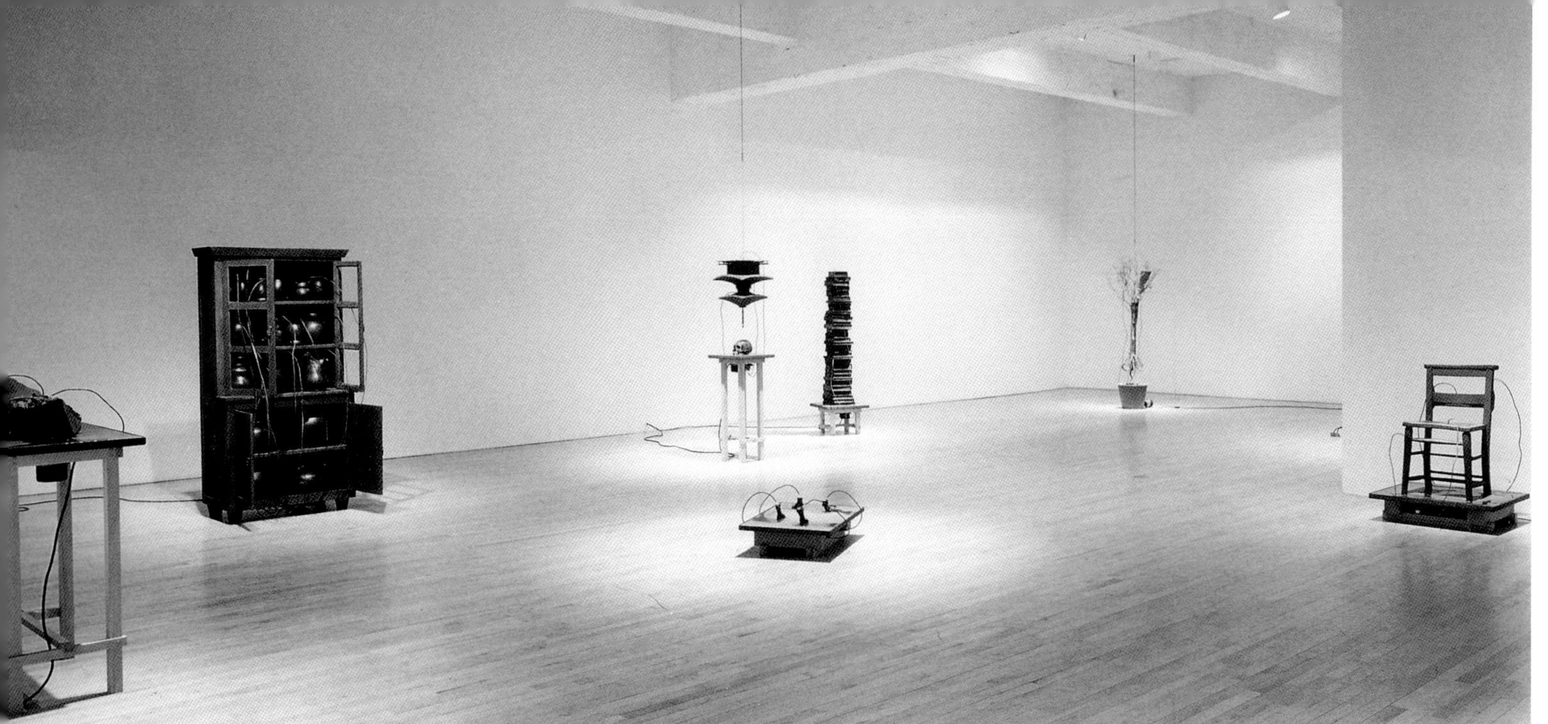

Figure 24
thingsgetwet, 1989–94
Bronze, water, copper, pumps, and wood
Dimensions variable
Installation view (1993), Louver Gallery, New York City

The idea of a collection of objects, exemplified on a macro-scale by complete installations such as **thingsgetwet** (fig. 24) and on a micro-scale by individual elements of **thingsgetwet** (fig. 25) or by earlier works such as **swordbasket** of 1978–79 (fig. 26) and **trunknuts** of 1982 (fig. 27), has long been important for Shelton:

> *I often work with this idea of a collection of gestures or a collection of forms or a collection of references that then becomes a kind of mandala.*[14] *At any one time you're laying out a set of objects that cumulatively become a universe or metauniverse of possibilities. This model can be both a mirror for what is and an armature for our desires.*

Shelton has emphasized the importance of his personal experiences to his work. "I think one of the criteria for choosing any particular object [for **thingsgetwet**] was keeping it very close to home, in the sense that it's something I had some experience with." An understanding of the autobiographical references in **thingsgetwet** adds to but is not necessary for the viewer's appreciation of the work.

The lack of a fixed narrative, or a "right" reading, is important to the success of **thingsgetwet** as a work of art. For Shelton closure is equated with smallness of mind and of purpose, and the open-endedness and multiplicity of interpretations offered by **thingsgetwet** defy what the artist has called "closing out." Yet these objects are hardly mute or without meaning for either the artist or the viewer.

14 A mandala is "a diagram designed to make clear the relationships between various deities or to outline a particular cosmogony in visual form.... Mandalas are combinations of both representation and an extreme form of symbolism, everything being arranged according to a rational scheme and presenting certain relationships." Sherman E. Lee, *A History of Far Eastern Art* (Englewood Cliffs, New Jersey: Prentice-Hall; New York: Harry N. Abrams, n.d. [1964]), pp. 288–93.

Often circular in form or combining a square and a circle, mandalas are composed of a large number of smaller, more intricate images. The great Buddhist monument Borobudur is often referred to as a very large mandala in stone. A mandala can also be seen as a meta-body, a paradigm for a living organism's relationship to its varied and individually complex parts. Frequently mandalas are inscribed with footprints or other body images.

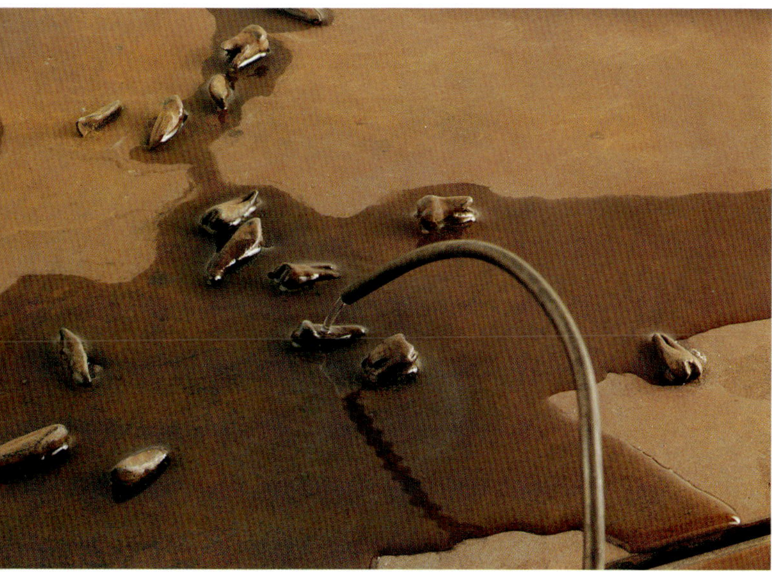

Figure 25
wetteeth, 1993
(detail)
from **thingsgetwet**, 1989–94
Bronze, water, copper, pump, and wood
36 x 30 x 19 1/2 in.
(91.4 x 76.2 x 49.5 cm)

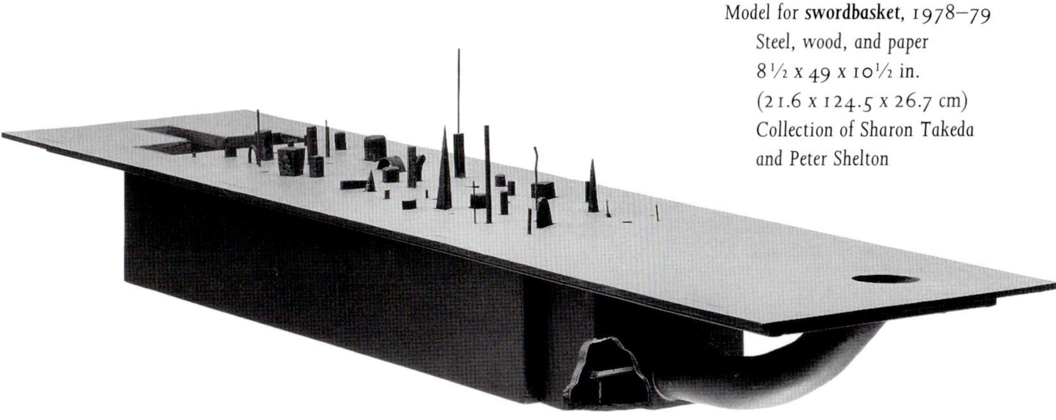

Figure 26
Model for **swordbasket**, 1978–79
Steel, wood, and paper
8 1/2 x 49 x 10 1/2 in.
(21.6 x 124.5 x 26.7 cm)
Collection of Sharon Takeda and Peter Shelton

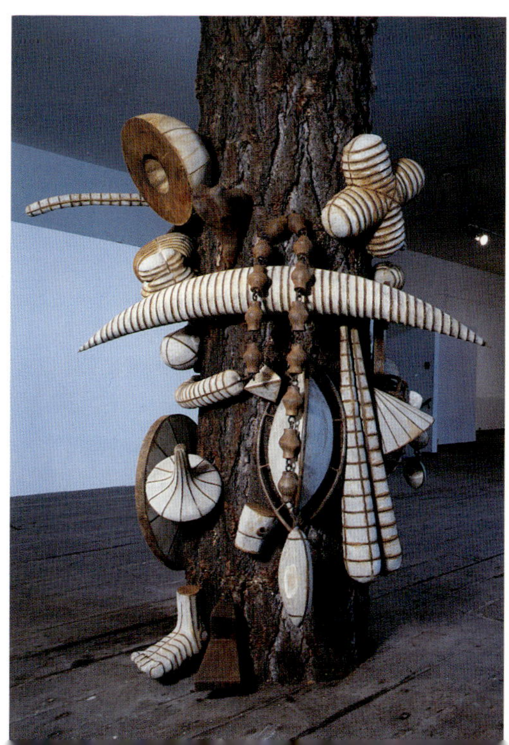

Figure 27
trunknuts, 1982
from **trunknuts WHITEHEAD floater**
Steel, cement, and tree trunk
height: 14 ft. (4.27 m);
diameter: 30 in. (76.2 cm)
Installation view, Open Space Gallery, Victoria, British Columbia

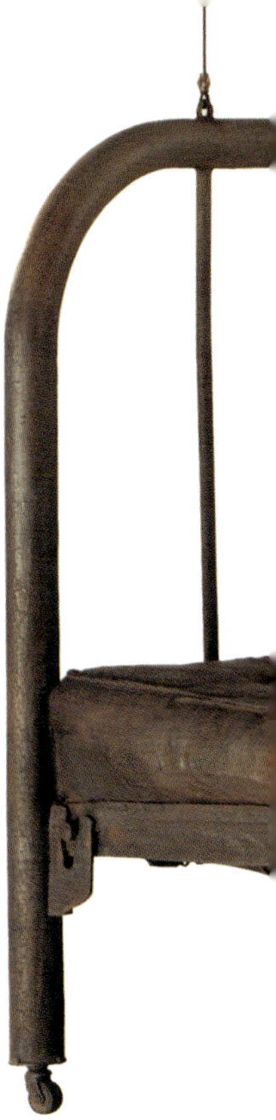

Figure 28
churchsnakebedbone, 1993
from **thingsgetwet**, 1989–94
Bronze, water, copper, and pumps
80 x 77 x 38 in.
(203.2 x 195.6 x 96.5 cm)

In **churchsnakebedbone** (fig. 28) we see that Shelton's interest in architecture as sculpture, his fascination with inverted and often ironic layerings, and his frequent conflation of the organic and the inanimate are all evident. The church is a scale model of the Cathedral of Chartres, representative of the classic High Gothic cathedral informed by the spiritual and physical metaphors contained in its soaring yet load-bearing columns and buttresses as skeleton, and its ultrathin walls and magnificent stained-glass windows as skin. Aside from the figural metaphor, Shelton was moved by his experience of Chartres as a space to be walked through, as an architecture that leads you on a physical and spiritual journey akin to Borobudur. Ironically, this architectural monument has been reduced to a small sculptural element and hung upside down under a bed on which a rattlesnake lies coiled (fig. 29). The snake is what Shelton, referring to his Arizona childhood, calls "a piece of boyhood mythology—cold, legless, utterly earthbound." The cathedral is doubly inverted, turned upside down and placed beneath the snake—the lofty Christian ideal below the base, cold-blooded animal, harking back to HEADROOM **footspace**.

The parallel placement of the human thigh bone and the leg of the bed suggests a latent animism reinforced by the dream references of the bed. The hard metal bedstead serves as a skeleton, and the "soft" mattress, now cast in bronze—another of Shelton's witty reversals—as flesh. The weight of the church pulls down on the bedsprings underneath the mattress creating teats, which strengthen the sense of **bed** as a living organism with its own corporeality.

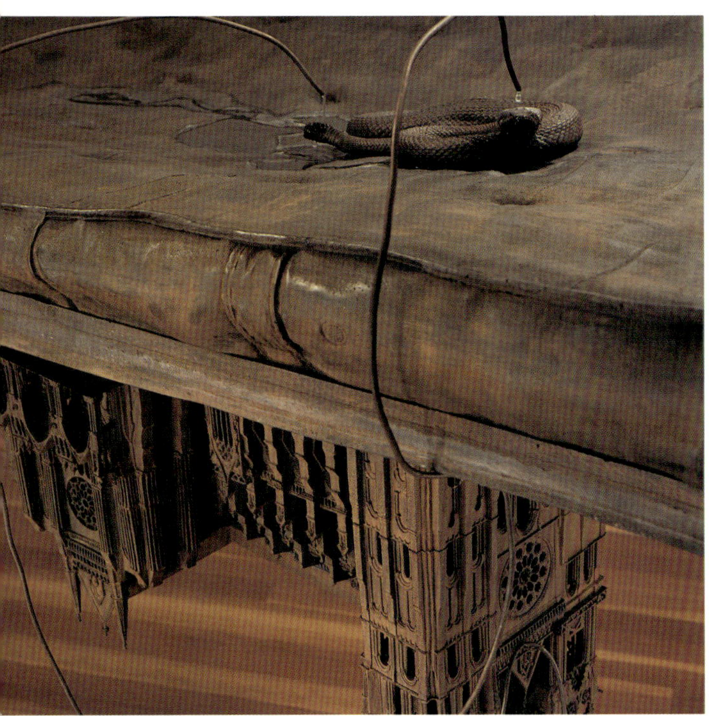

Figure 29
churchsnakebedbone, 1993
detail, **snake** and **church**

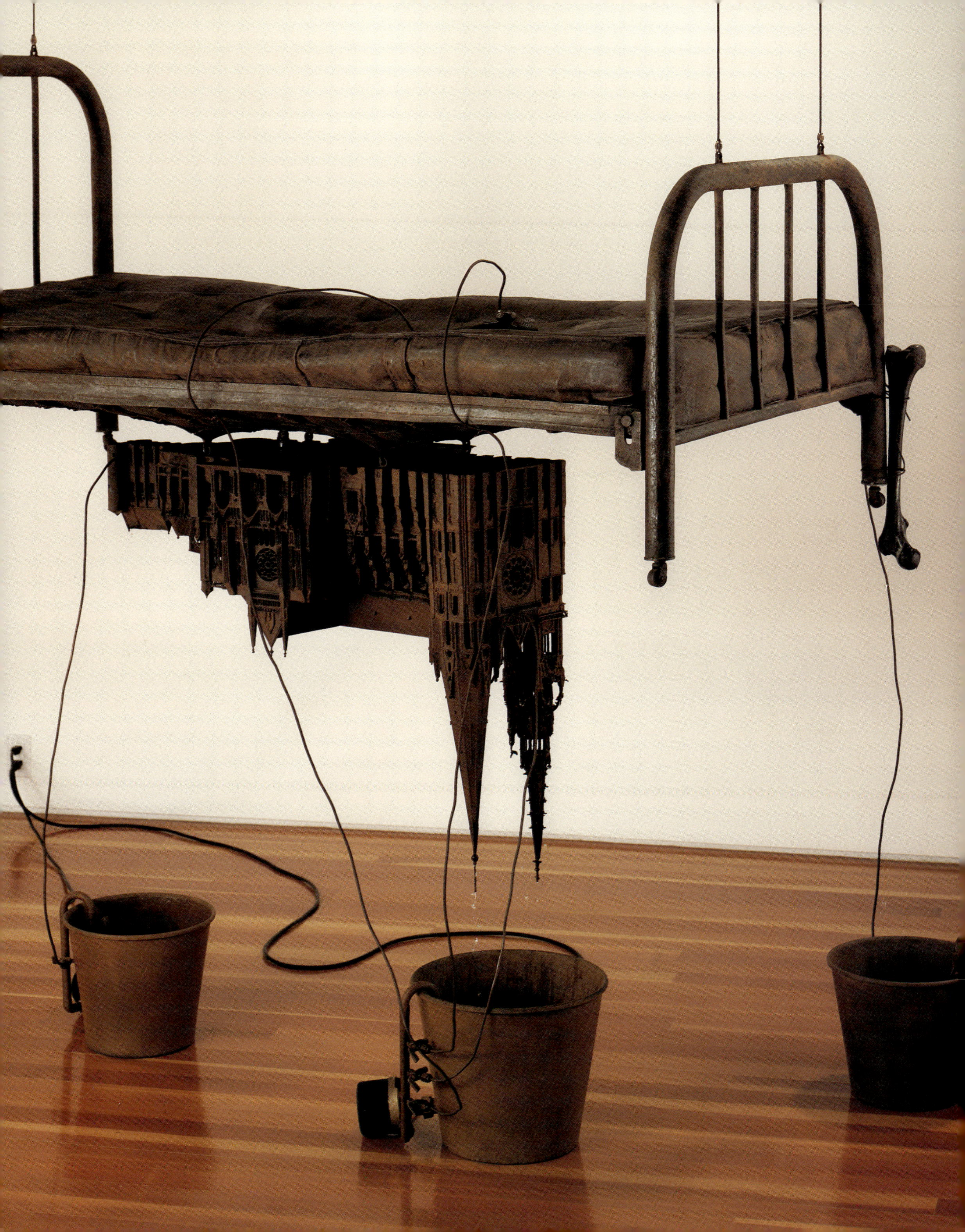

As in **churchsnakebedbone**, **pagodawindowskull** (fig. 30) combines architecture and human referents, again reflecting many of the themes of Shelton's work. **pagoda** (fig. 31) is an amalgam of two one-step pagodas in Japan: one, a large example in Ishiyamadera outside Kyoto, and the other, a very small pagoda in the monastery of Kongōsanmaiin in Kōyasan, a "beautiful mix between architecture and sculpture." The architectural form again is inverted and treated as a sculptural object; and, as in **church**, "it is an extraordinary skeletal structure, almost all skeleton with a kind of skin." Far from its original architectural function as a temple or a memorial to the dead, **pagoda**, "instead of focusing essences into the sky above it, here condenses gravity-bound water into our material body below, ironically, into a room [**windowskull**] that houses the immaterial mind" (fig. 32).

Most of the objects depicted in **thingsgetwet** have both personal and broader cultural meanings for Shelton. This is especially true of **windowskull**. Shelton's father was wounded while fighting in Belgium during World War II, and as a result, "has a big hole in his head that is covered by a tantalum [metal] plate. It's hard not to associate this skull with my father. But I look at it in broader terms, too." **windowskull** is based on a cast of an ancient Peruvian trephined skull that may have been cut open for medical reasons. Shelton sees this as "Western, materialistic, casual evidence of thinking that you should cut your head open and fix your brain and [close] it up again. We think that's the way everything gets done." In contrast, Shelton admires what he considers an Eastern approach:

> *Other cultures don't operate that way at all and don't view the body as a piece of meat to cut up and fool with and rearrange at will. [When] somebody dies, you know there's a reason for it. It's too simplistic to ascribe only a mechanical cause; it may have more to do with a natural order of things, some spiritual relationship that had to be appeased or related to or transformed.*

pagodawindowskull thus combines both Eastern and Western approaches to culture and to life cycles, mirroring what Shelton refers to as his materialistic, scientific, atheistic (i.e., Western) background combined with his interest in Eastern architecture and religions.

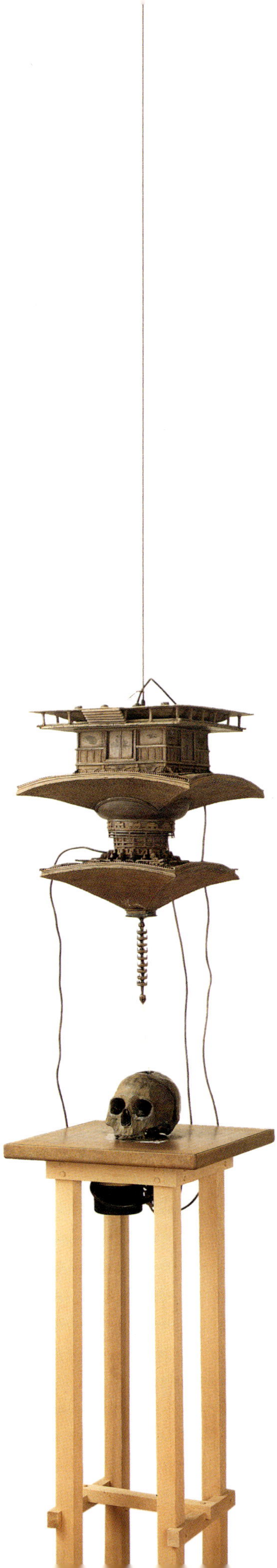

Figure 30
pagodawindowskull, 1993
from **thingsgetwet**, 1989–94
Bronze, water, copper, pump, and wood
68 x 16 x 16 in.
(172.7 x 40.6 x 40.6 cm)

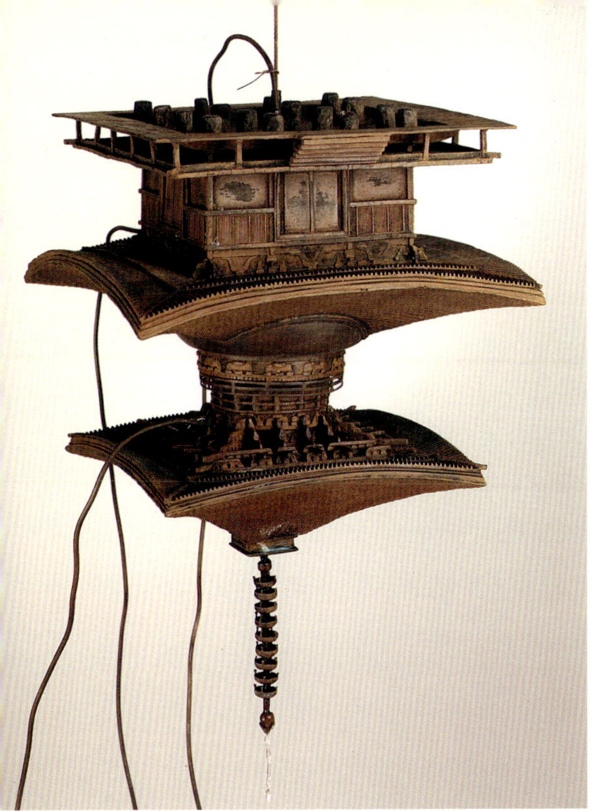

Figure 31
pagodawindowskull, 1993
detail, **pagoda**

Figure 32
pagodawindowskull, 1993
detail, **windowskull**

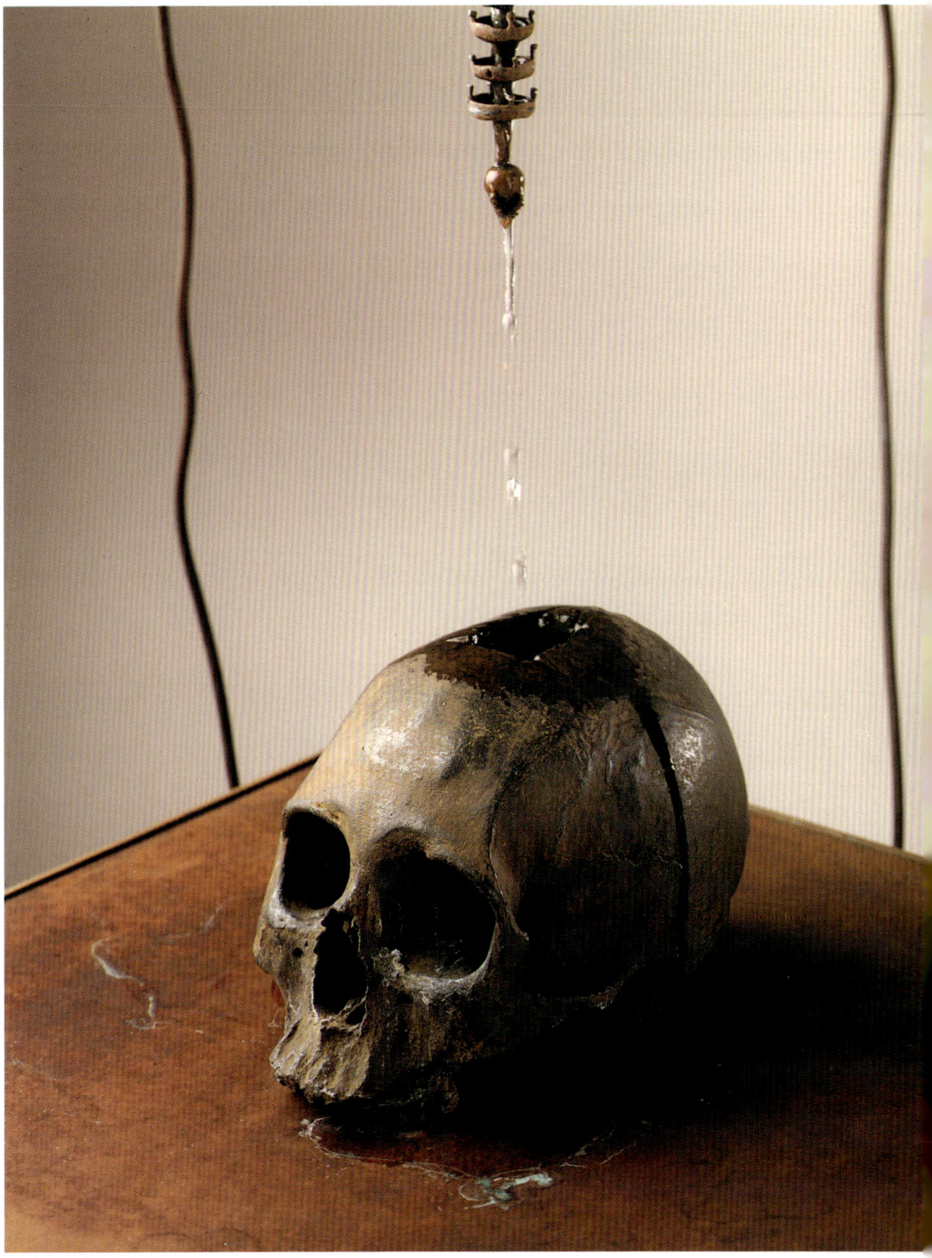

Figure 33
shotguncanetree, 1993
from **thingsgetwet**, 1989–94
Bronze, water, copper, and pump
76 x 27 x 21 in.
(193 x 68.6 x 53.3 cm)

Figure 34
shotguncanetree, 1993
detail, **cane**

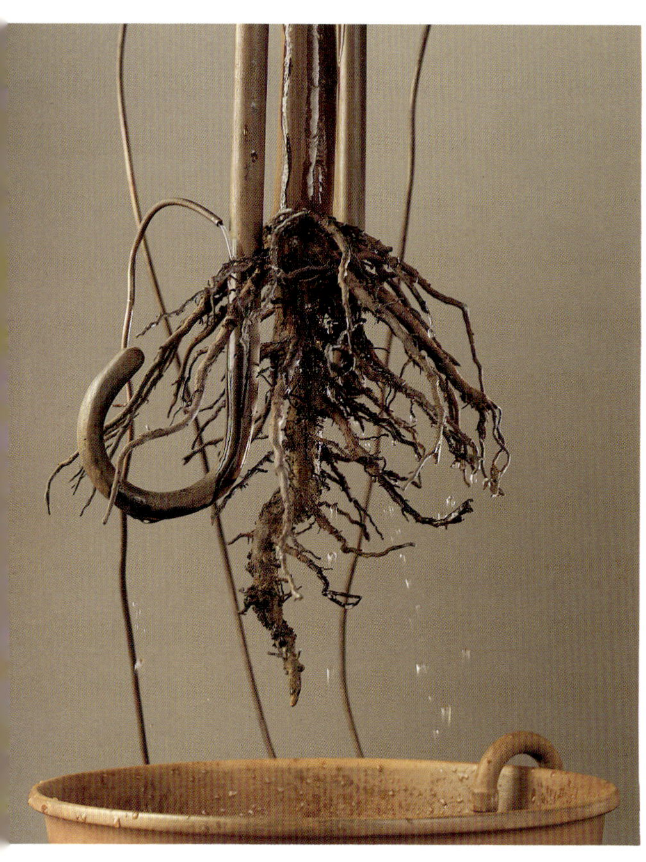

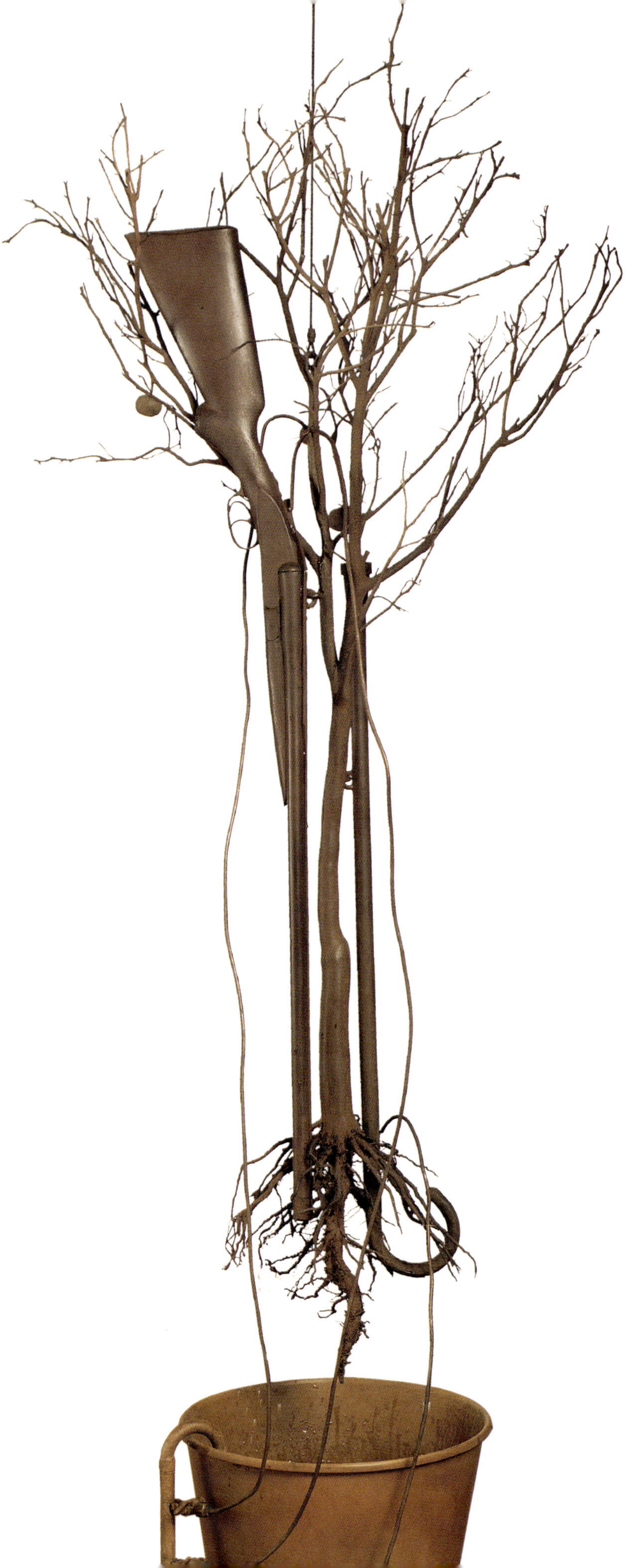

windowskull is a literal representation, while both the sculpture **pagoda** and a pagoda itself are highly metaphorical.[15] Shelton sees his work as a bridge between cultures as typified by approaches or styles. His work is hard and literal and material, but it is also ethereal and spiritual and conceptual.

shotguncanetree (fig. 33) similarly has personal as well universal references and meanings. **cane** (fig. 34) was cast from Shelton's father's cane in another reference to his World War II injuries. Typically Shelton has placed it upside down, thereby negating—even perverting—its function. The gun from which **shotgun** (fig. 35) was cast originally belonged to the artist's paternal grandfather, an avid hunter who grew up in the mountains of southern Ohio. Shelton himself had coveted the gun; as a child in Arizona he wanted it for hunting, and as an adult he valued it for sentimental reasons. The gun had become a symbol, specifically, a symbol of Shelton family history, and more generally, a symbol of patriarchal roles and power.

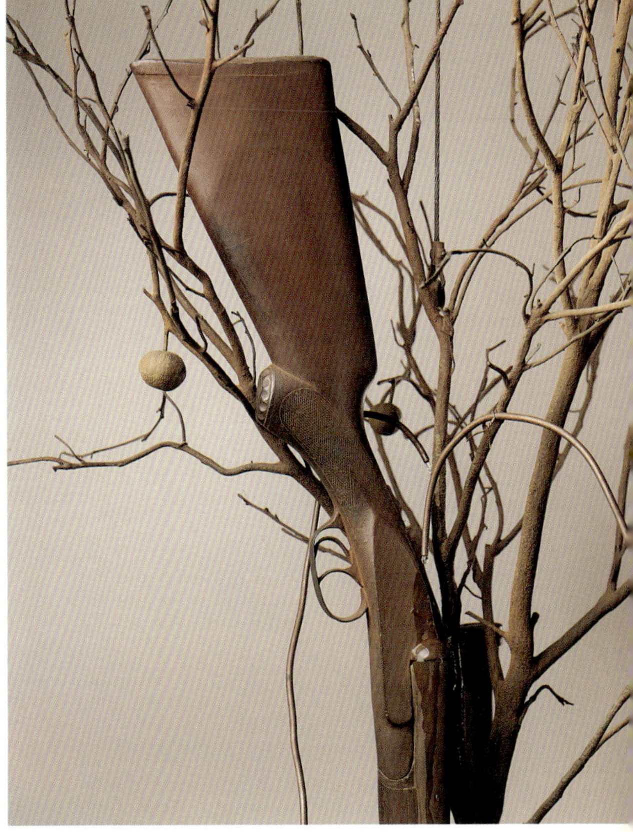

Figure 35
shotguncanetree, 1993
detail, **shotgun**

tree, with its bare branches, save for a few fruits, and exposed roots, likewise functions on many levels.

> *The tree is a mandarin orange tree. That was significant for me because in Arizona very little grew. We had one very pitiful tree in the backyard, which never yielded much, but it was always of great concern to my father. He was always talking about how sad this tree was. We played a practical joke on him where we pinned a grapefruit to this barren tree. He came in totally animated because fruit appeared on this tree overnight. A tree that wasn't supposed to bear grapefruit suddenly had fruit… he was very excited! Of course, he would only find out that he'd been had.*

With its multiple references to Shelton's father and grandfather, **shotguncanetree** becomes a family tree of sorts, a figurative homage to the artist's roots. On a more universal

---

15 The pagoda incorporates the earlier architectural form of the Indian stupa, originally a solid reliquary mound or tumulus, which metaphorically embodied not only the idea of death but also the idea of Buddha's transcendence. The stupa's form also refers to the womb and the ovum.

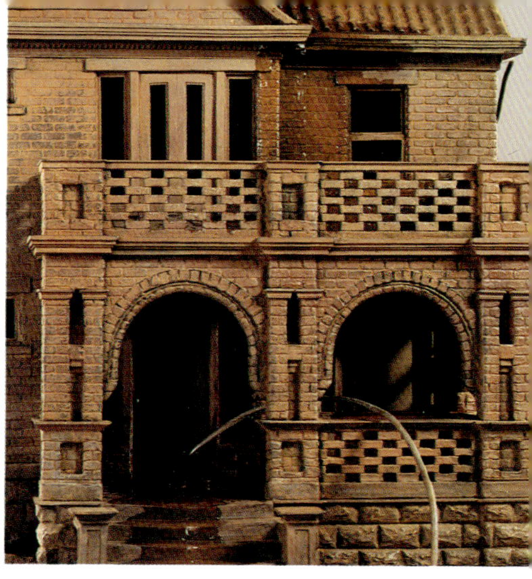

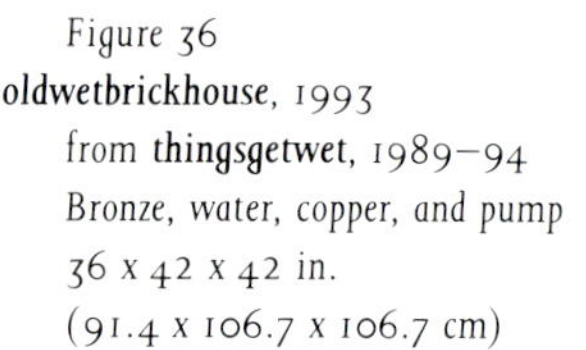

Figure 36
oldwetbrickhouse, 1993
from **thingsgetwet**, 1989–94
Bronze, water, copper, and pump
36 x 42 x 42 in.
(91.4 x 106.7 x 106.7 cm)

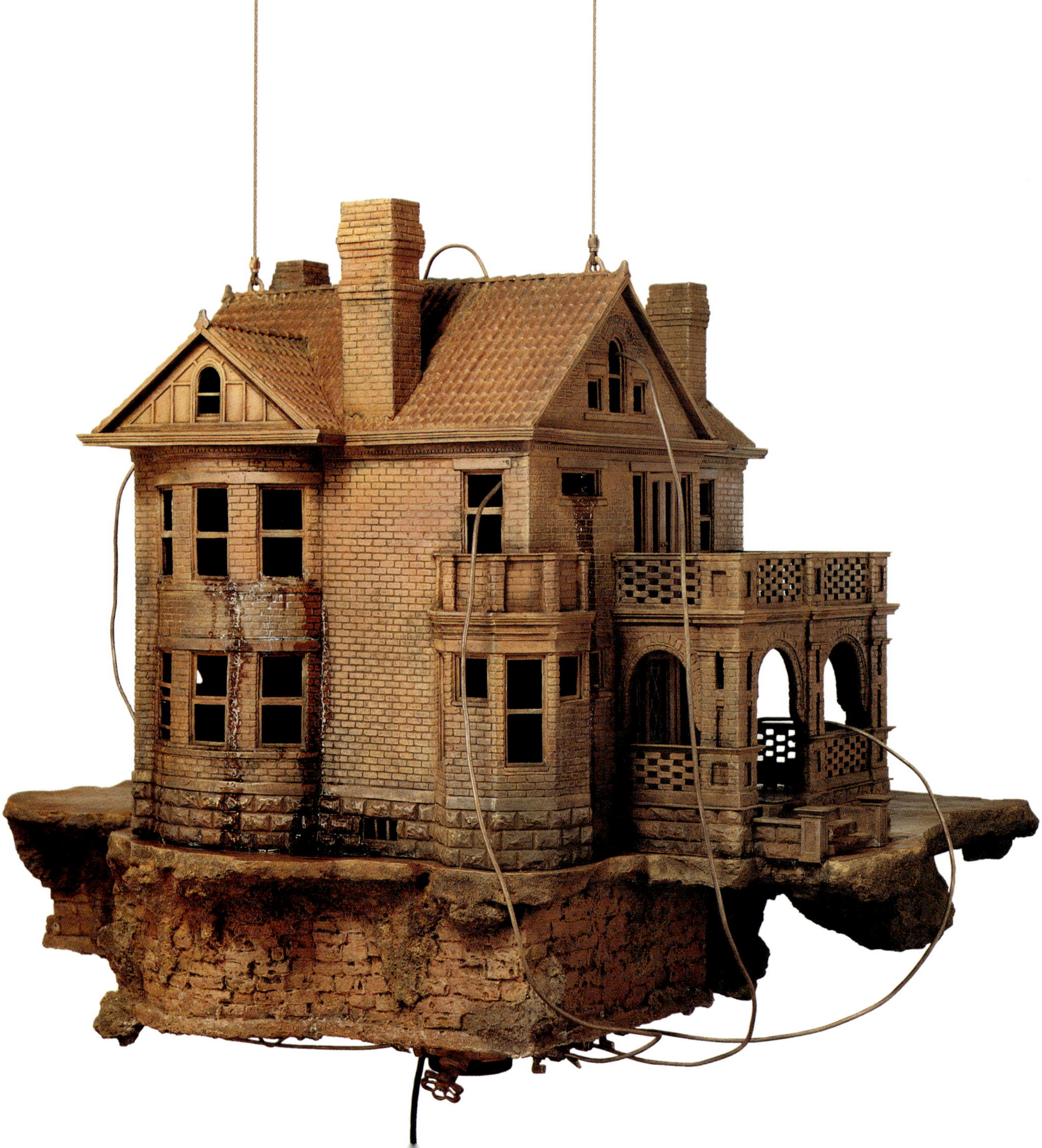

Figure 38
oldwetbrickhouse, 1993
(detail)

level, the leafless tree, with its few rather pitiful and isolated fruits, is an image of desolation and death. This is reinforced by **cane**, connoting old age, and **shotgun**, suggesting destruction.

Creating **oldwetbrickhouse** (fig. 36) was for Shelton a direct examination of his personal and artistic roots. The house, depicted along with its foundations and related incrustations, is Shelton's grandparents' house in Troy, Ohio (fig. 37), which he knew as a child and again when he returned to the Midwest. The sculpture is clearly an important touchstone in relation to Shelton's many layered architectural structures.

With its diminutive scale and extraordinary level of detail (fig. 38), **oldwetbrickhouse** is reminiscent of a Victorian dollhouse. Its very literalness brings up important issues related to figurative sculpture. On the one hand, this is a straightforward model of a particular house. On the other, the fact that the house and the eyelets from which it is suspended as well as its foundations and attached rocks and dirt are all cast from the same material and are evenhandedly detailed and bathed in water, challenges the sculpture's literal quality. A work which at first glance seems extremely accessible and comprehensible on further reflection becomes conceptually very complex. In this sense, **oldwetbrickhouse** is conceptually reminiscent of the Belgian surrealist René Magritte's seminal painting **The Treachery of Images** (fig. 39), which addresses head-on the issue of reality versus image. Shelton has, in fact, spoken of his admiration for Magritte's so-called word-image paintings.

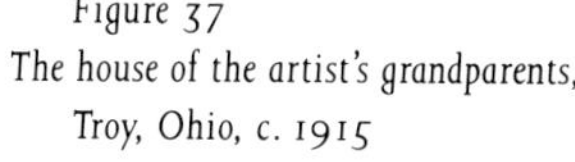

Figure 37
The house of the artist's grandparents,
Troy, Ohio, c. 1915

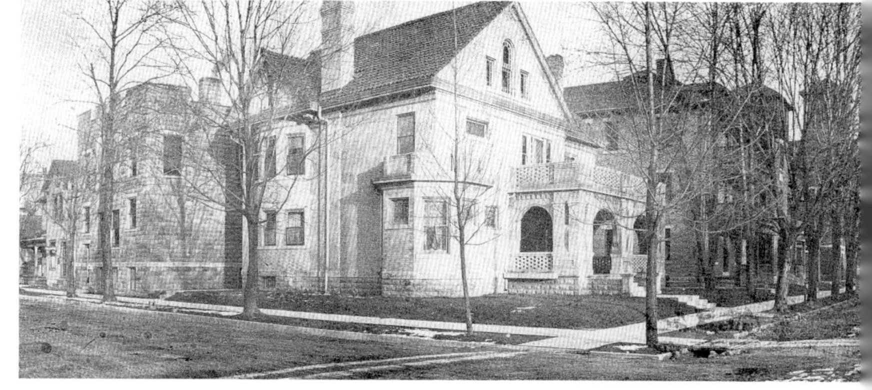

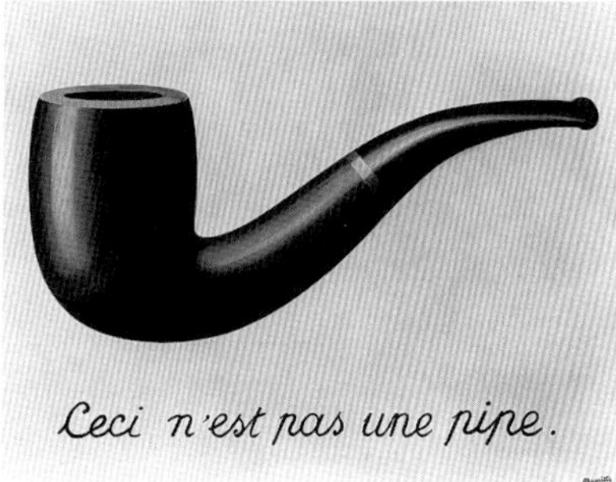

Figure 39
René Magritte
The Treachery of Images,
1928–29
Oil on canvas
21 1/2 x 28 1/2 in. (54.5 x 72.5 cm)
Los Angeles County Museum of Art, purchased with funds provided by the Mr. and Mrs. William Preston Harrison Collection

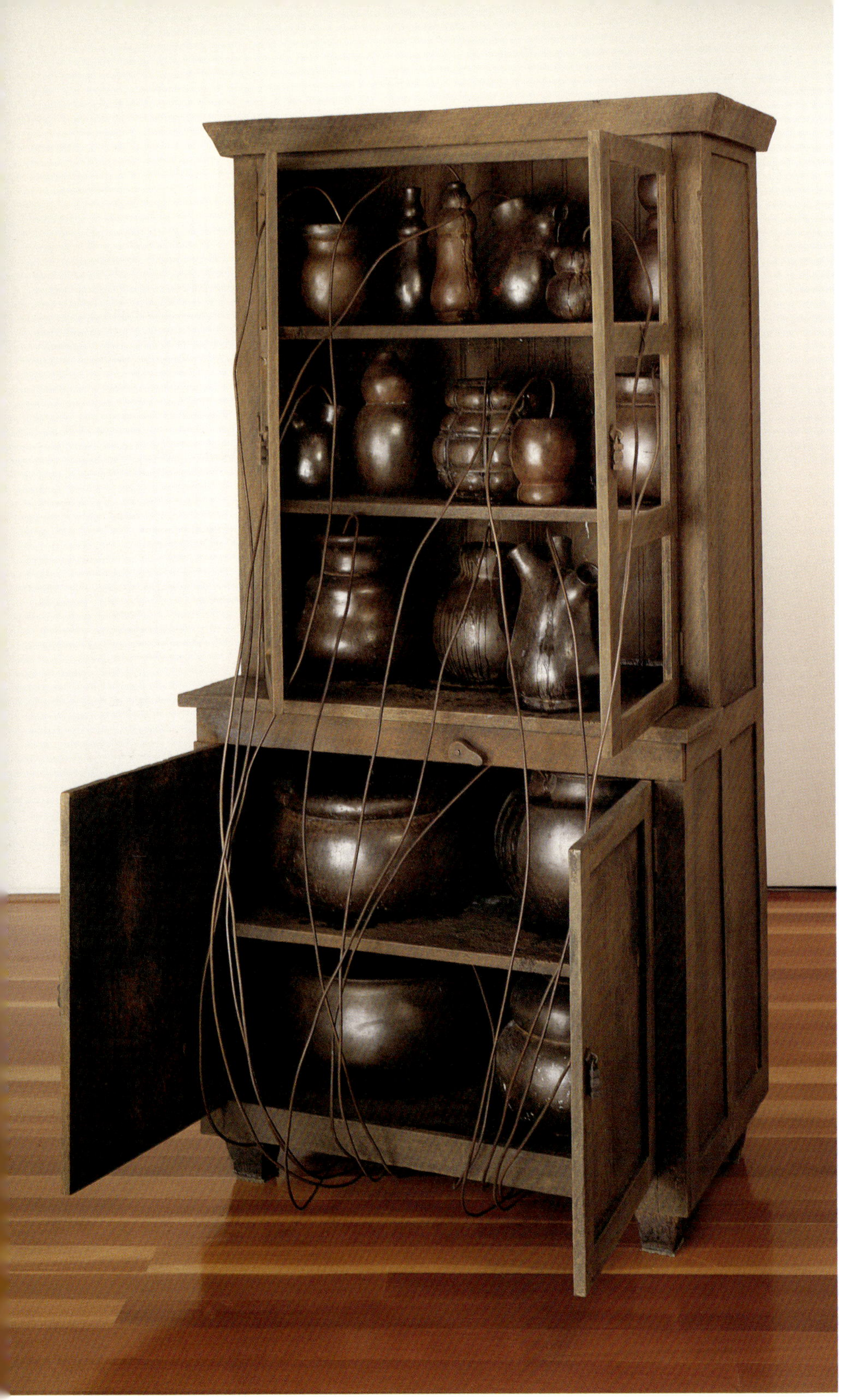

Figure 40
bowlshutch, 1993
from **thingsgetwet**, 1989–94
Bronze, water, copper, and pump
69 x 35 x 34 in.
(175.3 x 88.9 x 86.4 cm)

Figure 41
bowlshutch, 1993
detail, **bowls**

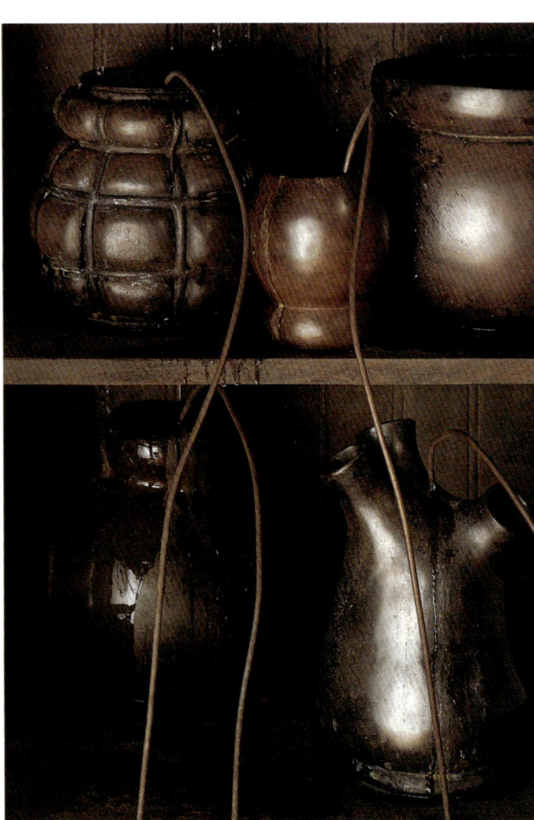

Figure 42
Female Figure Carrying a Pot
West Mexico, Jalisco,
c. 200 B.C.–A.D. 500
Clay with brown-gray slip
18 x 10¼ x 7½ in.
(45.7 x 26 x 19 cm)
Los Angeles County Museum of Art, the Proctor Stafford Collection, purchased with funds provided by Mr. and Mrs. Allan C. Balch

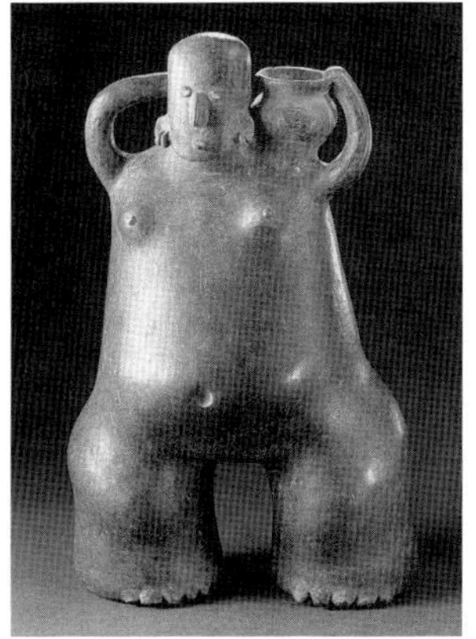

bowlshutch (fig. 40) is similarly both literal and evocative, both physically descriptive and conceptually abstracted, a paradigm of Shelton's concerns and interests. The artist likens it to "a nursery of little bodies or a carton of eggs. They're like seeds in a box. It's like a catalogue of different sculptures, only disguising themselves as conventional pots....Bowls become organs in a layered body complete with a vascular system." The contrast between the organic forms of **bowls** and the strict geometry of **hutch** serves to underscore the sense of oppositions and disguises in the work.

During Shelton's student years representation was anathema. In fact, he remembers being criticized at that time for the "latent figuration" present in much of his work. As a result, his figurative references have frequently been couched in abstracted or, at times, architectural terms. He has referred to the **bowls** (fig. 41) as "domesticated bodies which you think [are] about pots" based on the deceptive accessibility of their imagery. Just as pre-Columbian pots (fig. 42) are anthropomorphic, Shelton's **bowls** take on characteristics from various parts of the human anatomy: arms, bellies, necks.[16] **bottlemuff**, 1990–91 (fig. 43), foreshadows the conjoining of figural and vessel forms in **bowlshutch**, here on a large scale. Both **bottlemuff** and **bowlshutch** combine the figural and the architectural, harking back to works such as TUB and **blackdress**.

Other representations of inanimate objects in **thingsgetwet** likewise reflect Shelton's lifelong fascination with the forms and structure of the human body.[17] Of all the volumes piled up in **books** (figs. 44–45)—whose cast bronze spines are still, if barely, legible—the only one selected specifically for its subject matter was *Gray's Anatomy*.

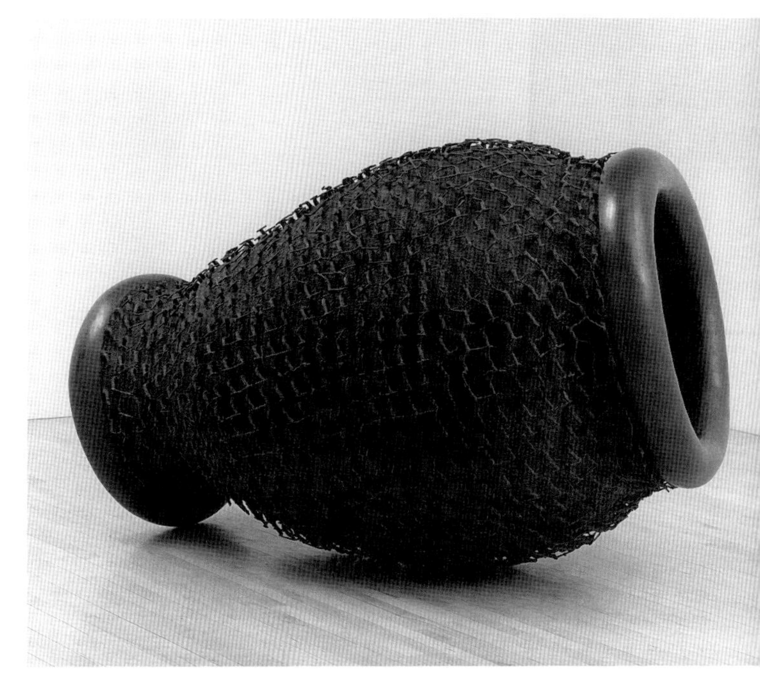

Figure 43
bottlemuff, 1990–91
Bronze
57 x 85 x 58 in.
(144.8 x 215.9 x 147.3 cm)
Private collection

16 Shelton has spoken specifically of his admiration for what he referred to as "the distorted and psychically altered bodies" in West Mexican pottery.

17 According to Peter Boswell, "By the time he reached the fifth grade, Peter Shelton knew the names of all the bones and muscles of the human body." ("Peter Shelton" in *Sculpture Inside Outside*, exh. cat. [Minneapolis: Walker Art Center; New York: Rizzoli, 1988], p. 217.)

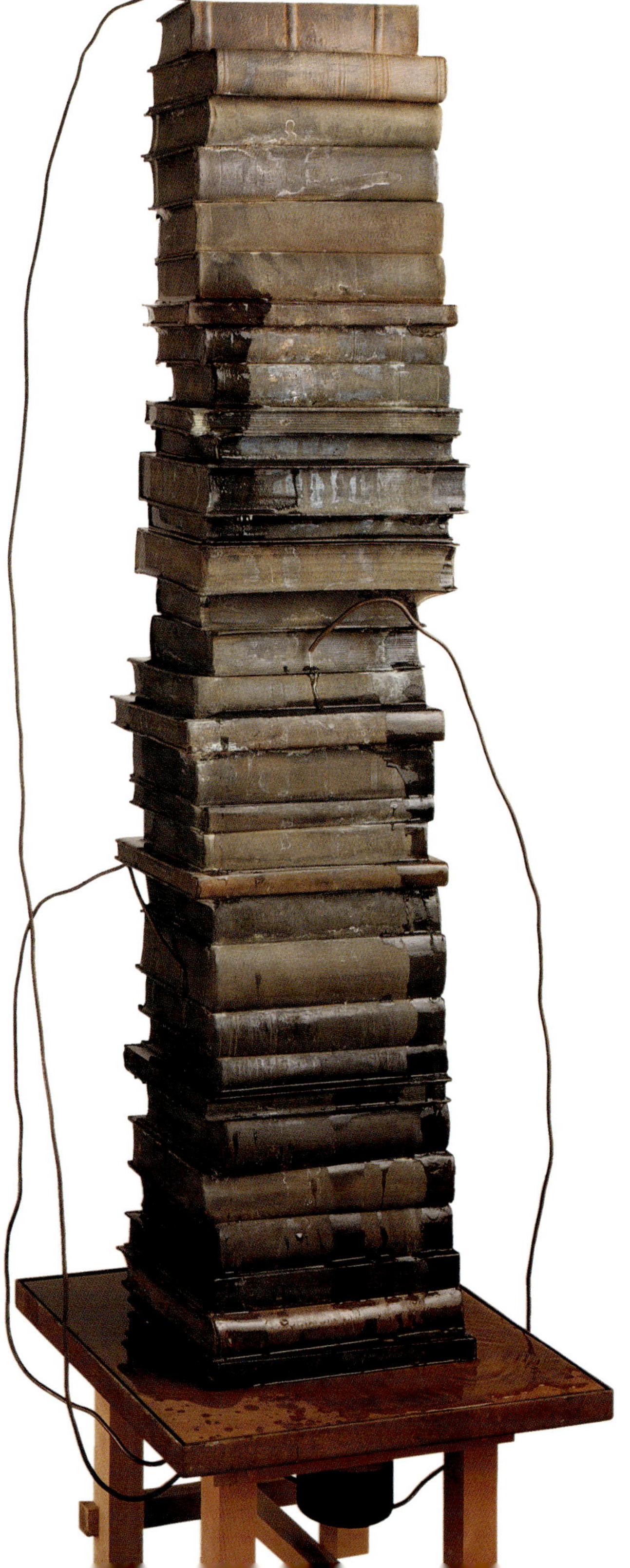

Figure 44
books, 1993
from **thingsgetwet**, 1989–94
Bronze, water, copper, pump, and wood
65 x 18 x 18 in.
(165.1 x 45.7 x 45.7 cm)

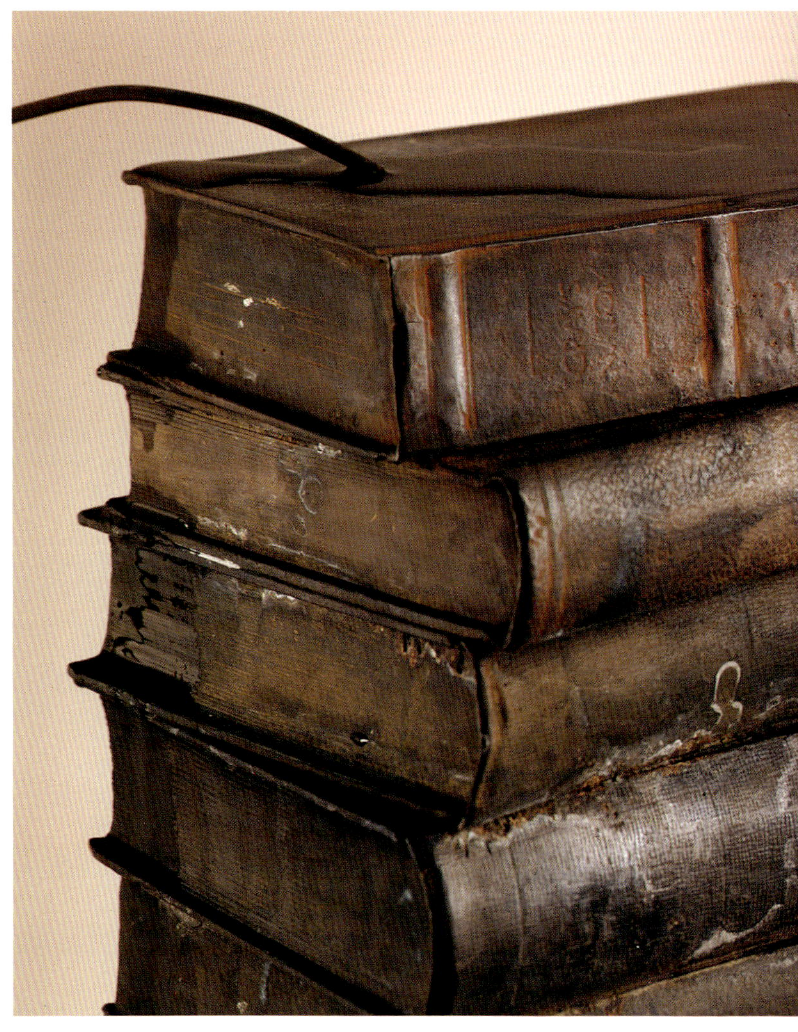

Figure 45
books, 1993
(detail)

The themes of Shelton's work recur frequently in other elements of **thingsgetwet**. A work such as **brain** (fig. 46) suggests ironic reversals. The traditional seat of logos and spirit, included earlier in **SWEATHOUSE and little principals** (fig. 47), is depicted here as a dangling cabbagelike form, disembodied and dysfunctional, literally with water on the brain. **brain** suggests that the perceived polarity between the conceptual or intellectual and the literal or physical can instead become a meaningful dialogue through the vocabulary of sculpture. **waterchair** (fig. 48), a Scottish church chair, has autobiographical references to Shelton's mother and grandmother, as does **blanket** (fig. 49) to his father. Just as he frequently conflates sculpture and architecture, in **blanket** Shelton conflates sculpture and landscape. The folded blanket becomes a metaphor for a gently terraced and slightly hilly plot of land. **log** (fig. 50) similarly conflates sculpture and landscape as well as the animate and inanimate. Shelton has referred to the log as an "elemental torso" that simultaneously has a "vaginal gash" and a "branching penis." In this case, the water serves to wash, heal, and purify a part of nature that has been brutalized.

In the many conduit and tube forms Shelton has made, water is suggested rather than literally present. He has repeatedly created forms that reflect "a pneumatic or hydraulic vessel, a collector or condenser, a passage in all its different scales, a 'tube' that you pass through, a tunnel, a hallway, a pipe. You could think of them in terms of a circulation system."

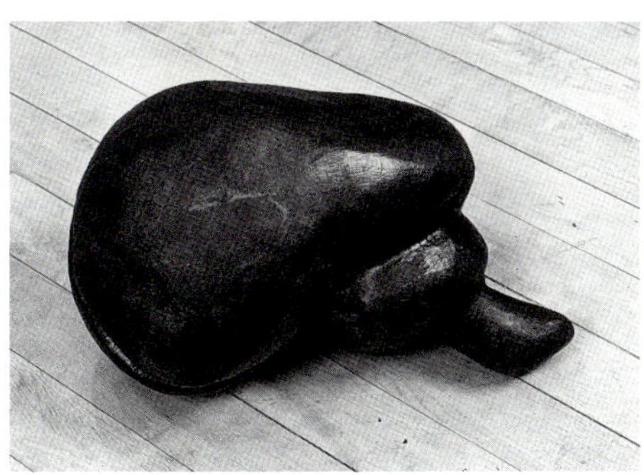

Figure 47
brain, 1982
from **SWEATHOUSE and little principals**, 1977–82
Steel
6 1/2 x 12 x 9 in.
(16.5 x 30.5 x 22.9 cm)

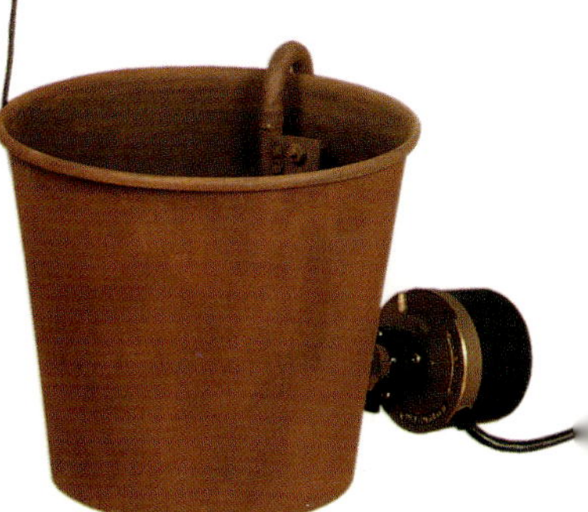

Figure 46
brain, 1989
from **thingsgetwet**, 1989–94
Bronze, water, copper, and pump
69 x 17 x 16 in.
(175.3 x 43.2 x 40.6 cm)

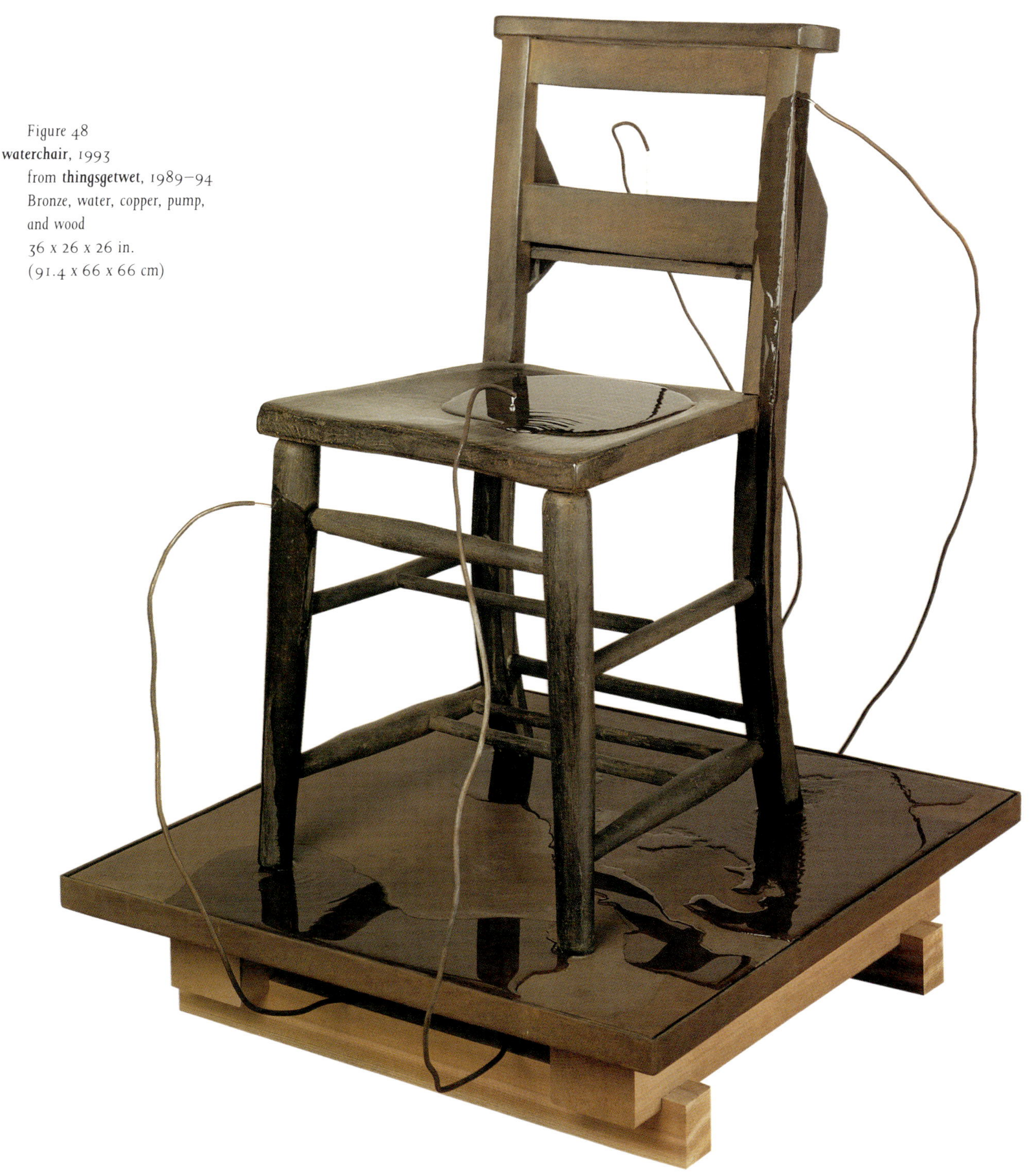

Figure 48
waterchair, 1993
from **thingsgetwet**, 1989–94
Bronze, water, copper, pump, and wood
36 x 26 x 26 in.
(91.4 x 66 x 66 cm)

Figure 50
log, 1993
(detail)
from **thingsgetwet**, 1989–94
Bronze, water, copper, pump, and wood
44 x 30 x 20 in.
(111.8 x 76.2 x 50.8 cm)

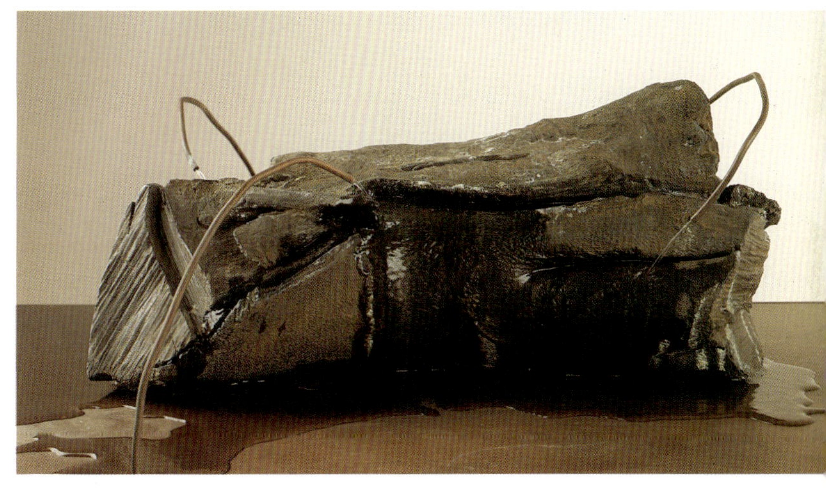

Figure 49
blanket, 1993
from **thingsgetwet**, 1989–94
Bronze, water, copper, pump, and wood
41 x 32 x 28 in.
(106.7 x 81.3 x 71.1 cm)

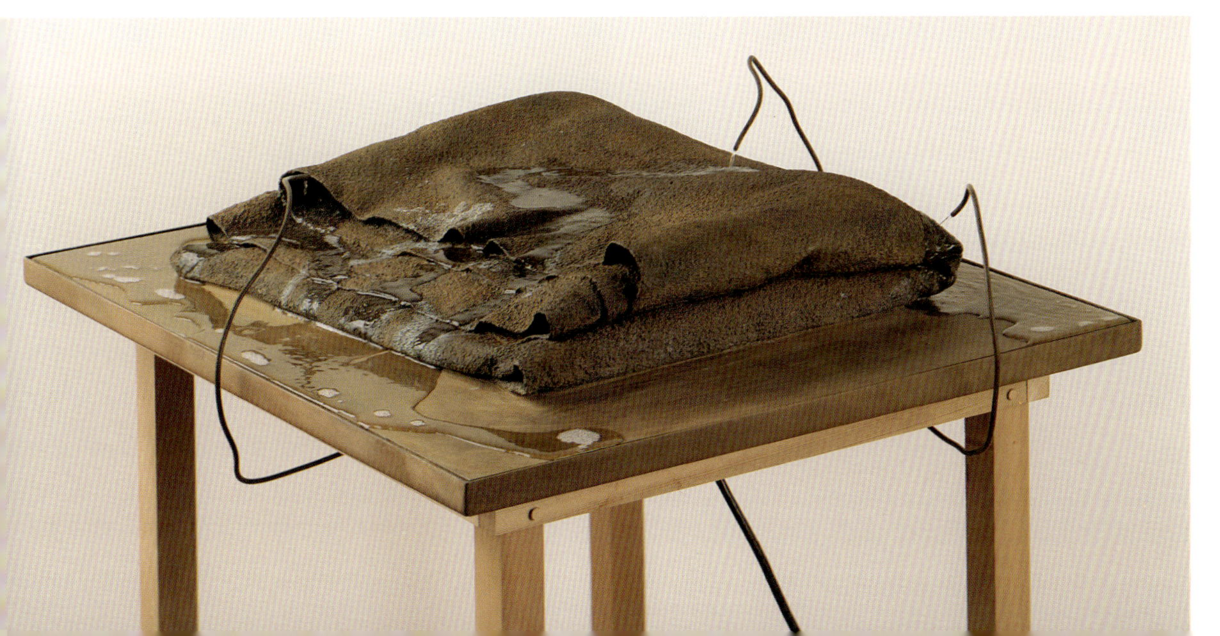

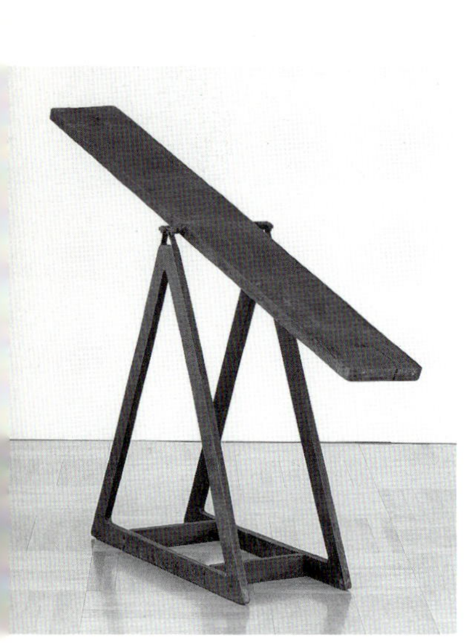

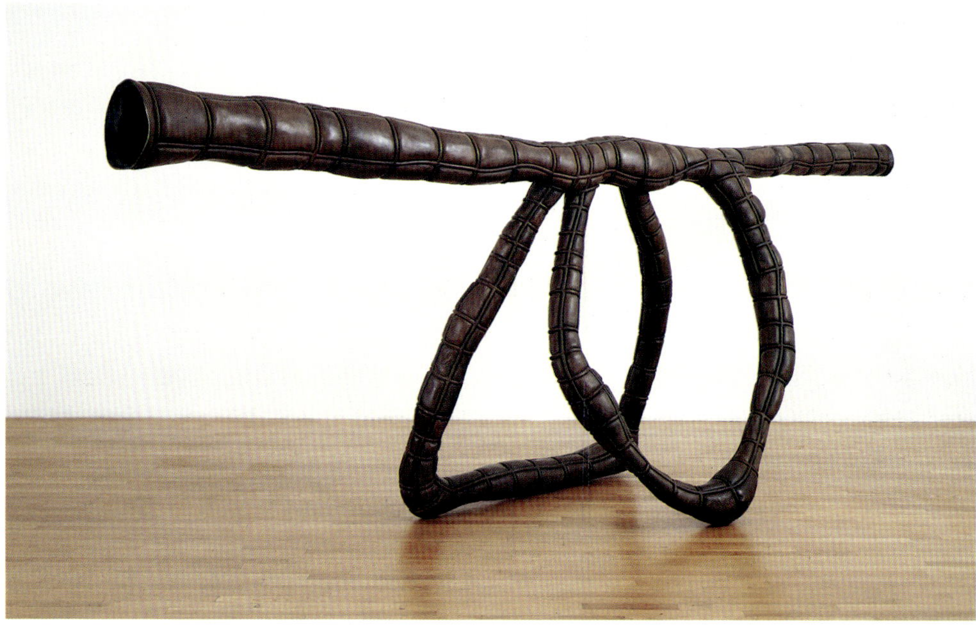

Figure 51
steamengine, 1975–76
Steel
96 x 66 in.
(243.8 x 167.6 cm)
Collection of Sharon Takeda
and Peter Shelton

Figure 52
horseheader, 1990–91
Bronze
62 x 148 x 48 in.
(157.5 x 375.9 x 121.9 cm)

Such references recur in various guises throughout Shelton's career (figs. 51–52), culminating in a work-in-progress titled **clearcuttubesandpipes** (figs. 53–55), which Shelton has described as "the boneyard of a vanished behemoth or perhaps the salvaged plumbing of some sublime architecture." Literally a catalogue of cast fragments of works made during the past eight to ten years, such as **blackmouthheader**, **u-bone with drain** (figs. 56–57), and **snakearm**, **clearcuttubesandpipes** defies the viewer's ability to gauge its scale or read its specific forms. Using a vocabulary of highly abstracted forms fabricated in fiberglass and lead, **clearcuttubesandpipes** conflates the animate and the inanimate, the architectural and the sculptural, the architectural and the anatomical. The multiplicity of references—everything from arteries to condensers to intestines to birth canals to plumbing pipes—is reflected in the multiplicity of individual forms that are always suggestive but never descriptive. The simultaneous allusions of any one element range from the organic to the mechanical: the birth canal to the sewage canal, torsos to mufflers, windpipes to exhaust pipes. The bone and skin references of the elements of **clearcuttubesandpipes**, with their smooth, translucent fiberglass skins and lead wire exoskeletons, are ubiquitous. As with **thingsgetwet** and other works, Shelton here gathers many elements into a cohesive whole.

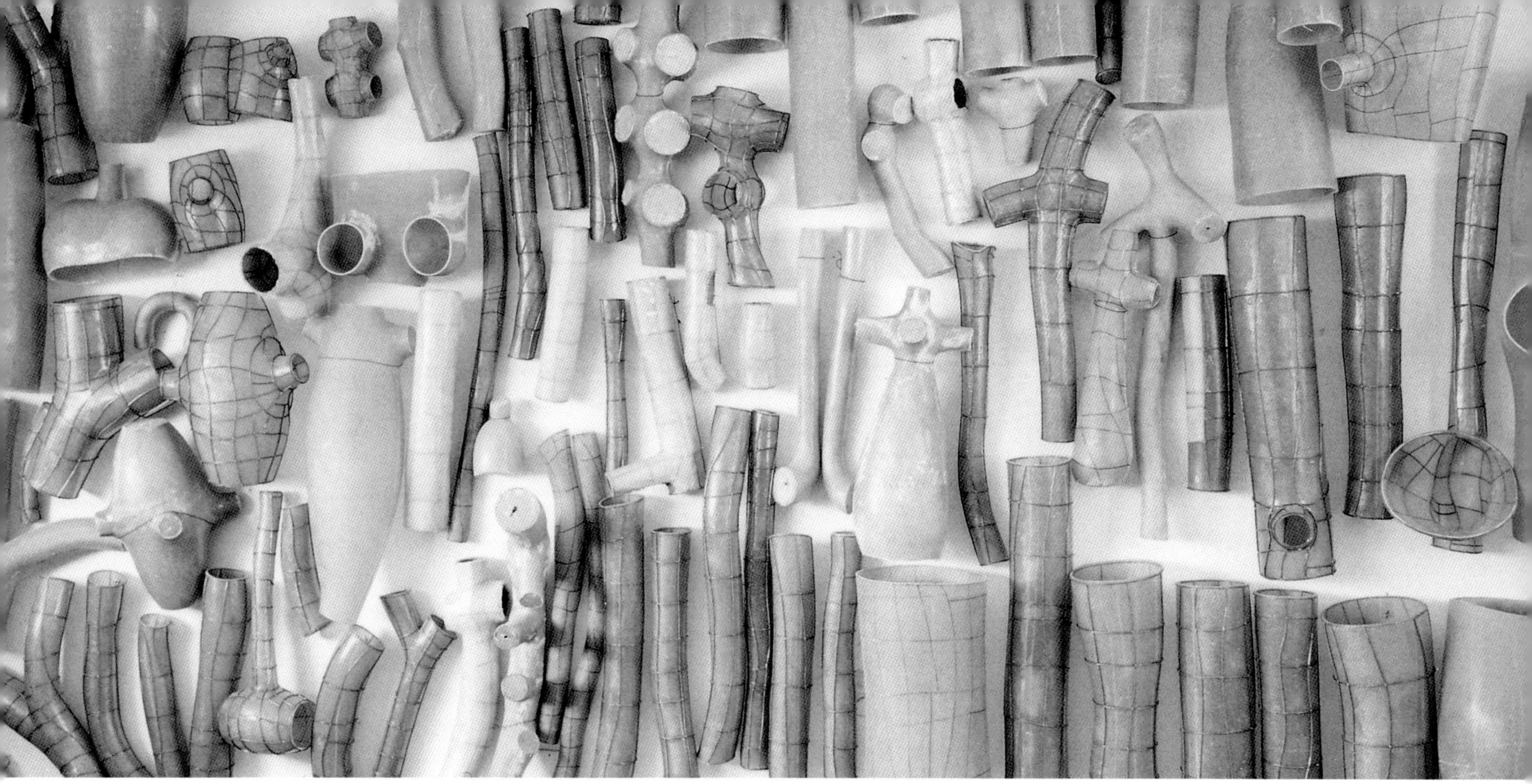

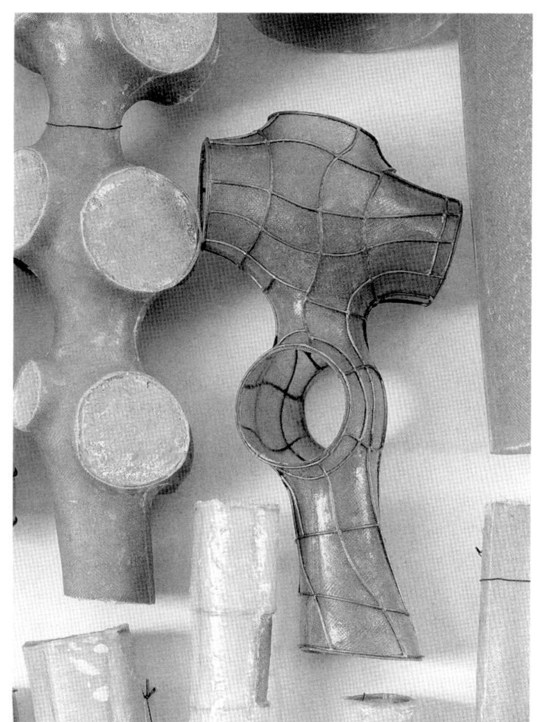

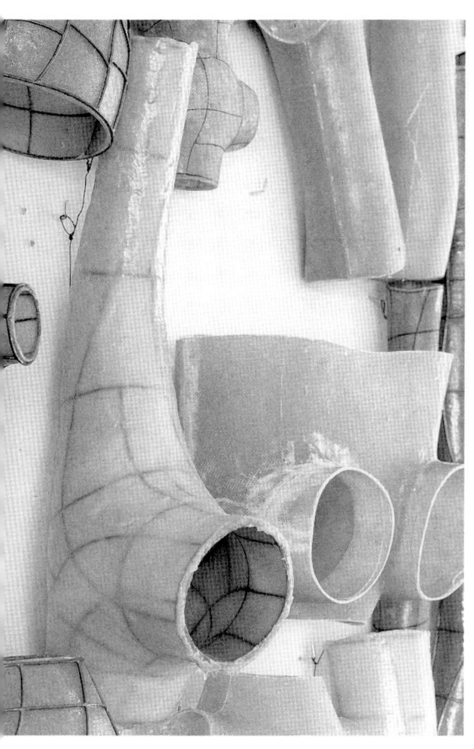

Figures 53–55
clearcuttubesandpipes,
work-in-progress
Mixed media
Dimensions variable

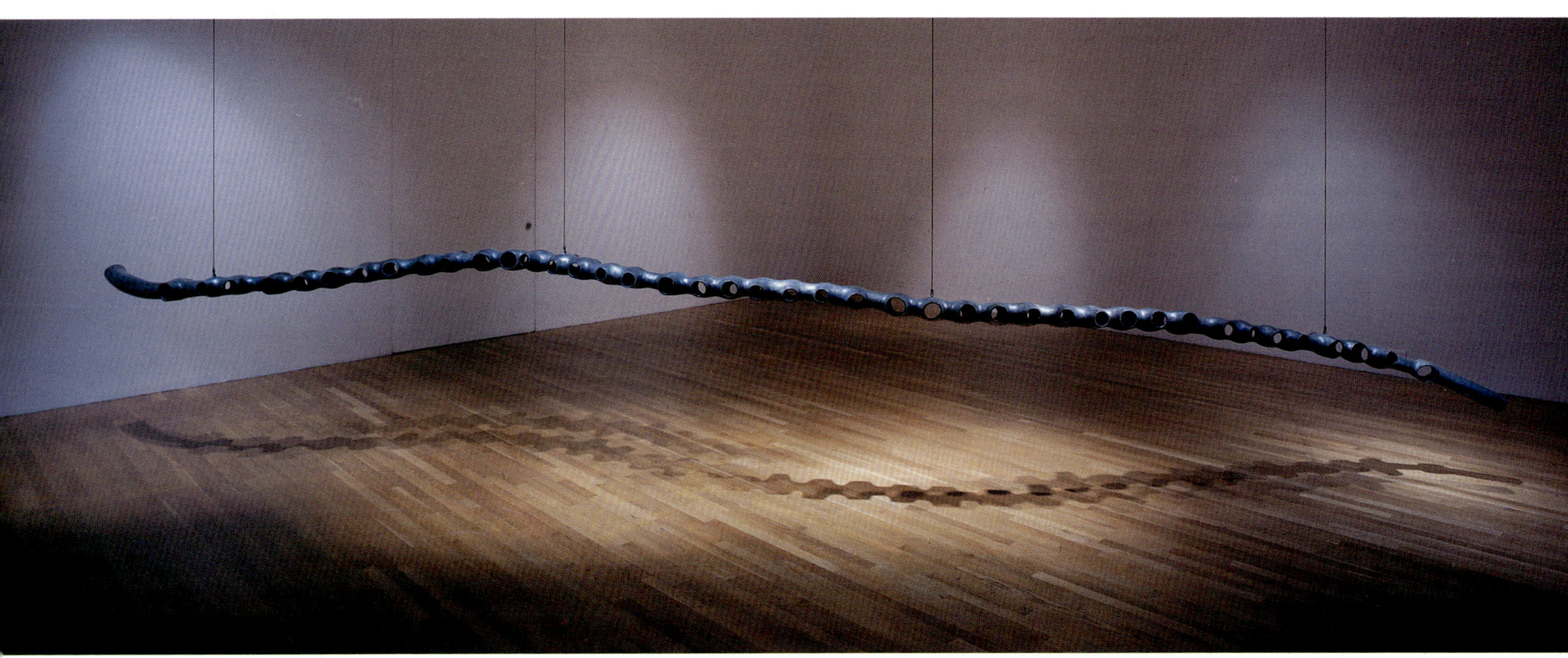

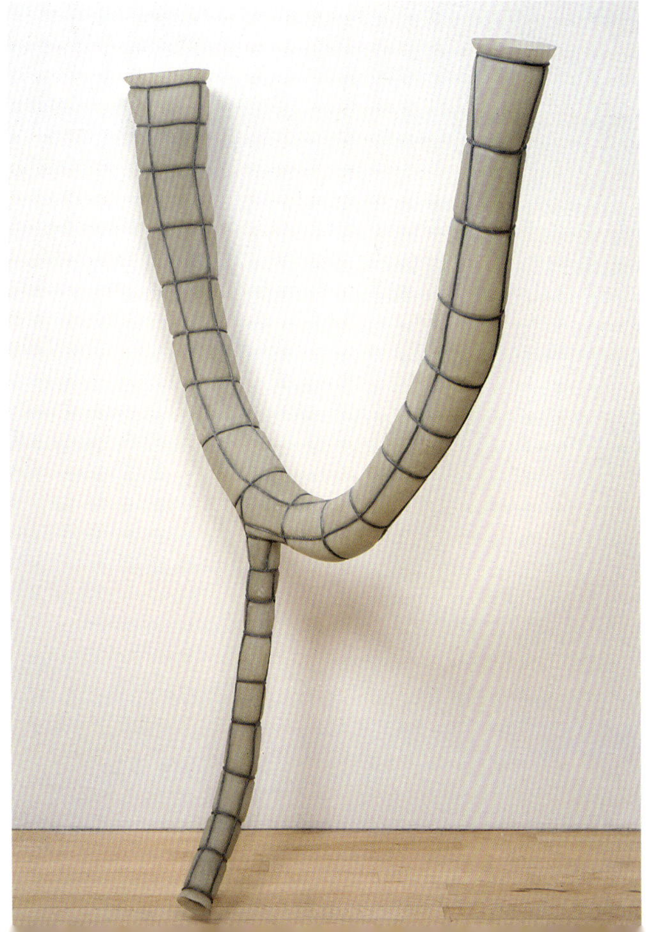

Figure 56
blackmouthheader, 1987–89
Bronze
4 1/2 x 283 x 8 in.
(11.4 x 718.8 x 20.3 cm)
Douglas S. Cramer Foundation

Figure 57
u-bone with drain, 1990–92
Mixed media
78 x 48 x 8 in.
(198.1 x 121.9 x 20.3 cm)

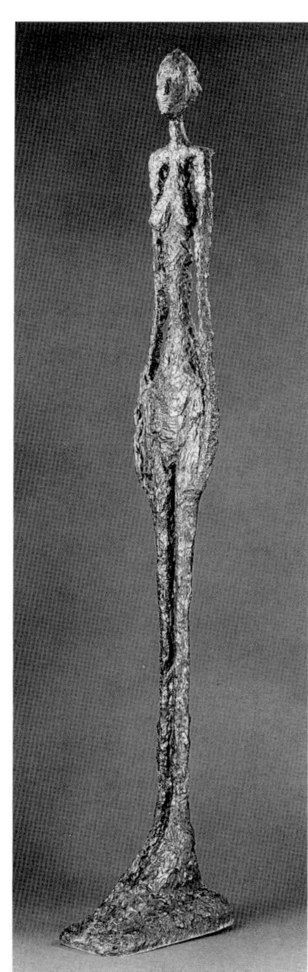

Figure 58
Alberto Giacometti
Large Standing Woman IV, 1960
Bronze
106 x 13 1/8 x 22 1/2 in.
(262.2 x 33.4 x 57.2 cm)
Los Angeles County Museum of Art, gift of Mr. and Mrs. David L. Wolper

In many ways Shelton's work stands apart from that of other artists. He has, however, spoken of his particular interest in and respect for a number of earlier artists. Alberto Giacometti was a sculptor who strove to combine the seen (the phenomenal), the known (the intellectual), and the felt (the intuitive) in his work. The tension among these ways of perceiving the world is clearly expressed in Giacometti's sculptures (fig. 58). While Shelton's formal vocabulary differs from Giacometti's, his desire to combine various modes of understanding the world is very similar.

Not only does Shelton share David Smith's midwestern roots, but he admires how Smith's interest in the pragmatic, physical aspects of creating sculpture become a part of the finished work: the way that elements are supported and the way that elements are welded together (fig. 59). The sense that Smith's body and gestures were carried into the work—the scale of a sculpture being dictated by the sculptor's reach—as well as Smith's creation of images such as **The Letter** (fig. 60), with an implied but ultimately unreadable narrative, jibe with Shelton's concept of the sculptor and his role as creator. The idea of a sculpture as a catalogue of individual elements, like Smith's **Home of the Welder** and Shelton's **clearcuttubesandpipes**, or an installation as a catalogue of sculptures, like the placement of Smith's works on his own property in Bolton Landing, New York (fig. 61), and Shelton's **thingsgetwet**, also links the two sculptors, as does their interest in the human figure without a focus on figuration per se (fig. 62).

As did Smith, Shelton also admires the great modernist sculptor Constantin Brancusi for his equal treatment of pedestal and sculpture, for his interest in a great variety of materials, and for his contrasts between the raw and the refined, between the abstract and the representational, and between the organic and the geometric (fig. 63).

Despite his keen awareness of art since the 1970s, Shelton's work is distinct from that of his contemporaries. Although Shelton greatly admires Bruce Nauman, who for many years has experimented with various ways to use his own body in his work and who has not been limited to any one formal method or one set style, Shelton's work is

Figure 60
David Smith
The Letter, 1950
Welded steel
37 5/8 x 22 7/8 x 9 1/4 in.
(95.6 x 58.1 x 23.5 cm)
Munson-Williams-Proctor Institute, Museum of Art, Utica, New York

Figure 59
David Smith
Home of the Welder, 1945
Steel
21 x 17 3/8 x 14 in.
(53.3 x 43.8 x 35.6 cm)
Tate Gallery, London, lent from the collection of Candida and Rebecca Smith, 1984

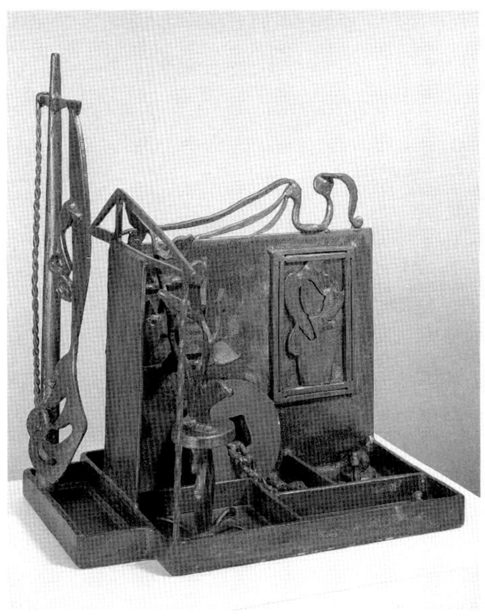

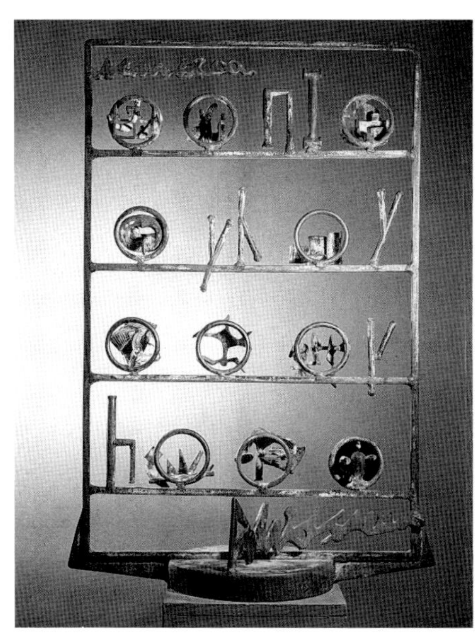

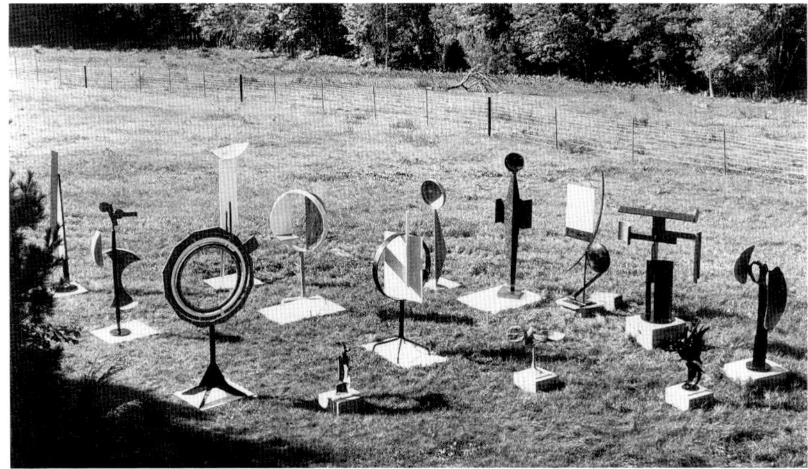

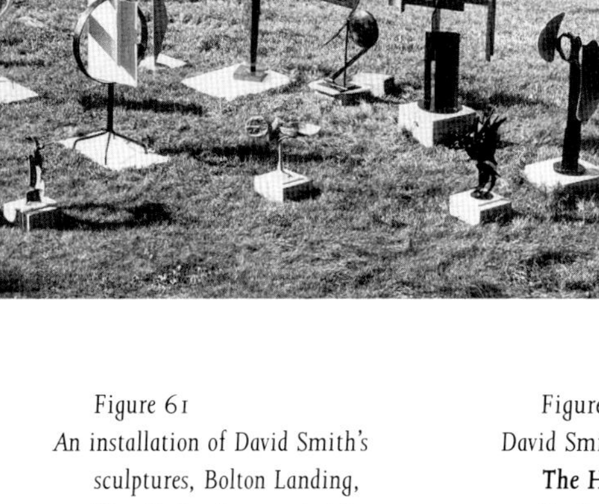

Figure 61
An installation of David Smith's sculptures, Bolton Landing, New York, photographed by David Smith
The David Smith Papers, on deposit at the Archives of American Art, Smithsonian Institution

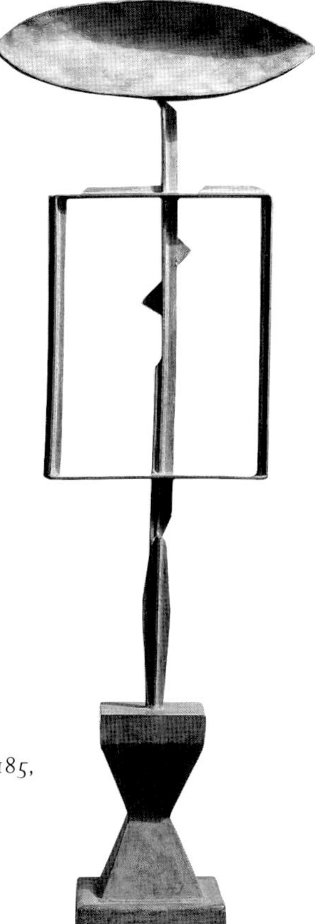

Figure 62
David Smith
The Hero, 1952
Steel
73 11/16 x 25 1/2 x 11 3/4 in.
(187.2 x 64.8 x 29.8 cm)
The Brooklyn Museum, 57.185, Dick S. Ramsay Fund

Figure 63
Constantin Brancusi
Sleeping Child, 1908
Marble on wood base
marble: 5 x 6 ½ x 5 ½ in.
(12.7 x 16.5 x 13.3 cm)
base: 21 ½ x 12 x 12 in.
(54.6 x 30.5 x 20.5 cm)
Nathan and Marion Smooke Collection

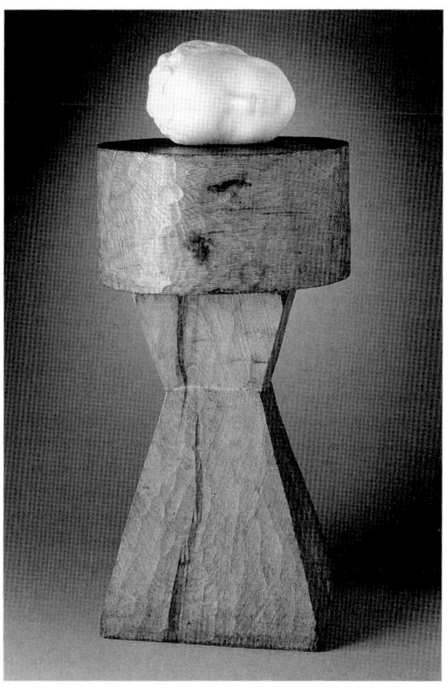

very different from Nauman's in both formal terms as well as in Shelton's ongoing preference for traditional materials. While one can draw various superficial formal parallels between Shelton's work and that of, say, Martin Puryear, Joel Shapiro, or others, ultimately Shelton's concerns are different. The ambiguities, seeming contradictions, enigmas, multiple layers (both literal and figurative), and conflations of both form and content in Shelton's work create a richness of meaning that rewards a slow and careful consideration of his sculpture.

Shelton himself has said, "What makes sculpture strong is that it deals in the most physical way with the least physical of things—ideas."[18] Unlike the mythological Galatea, whose beloved stone image by Pygmalion came to life through the divine intervention of Aphrodite, Shelton's works never literally come to life. Instead, he constantly breathes life into his own ideas, which are then transformed into physical reality.

18 Shelton, pp. 26–27.

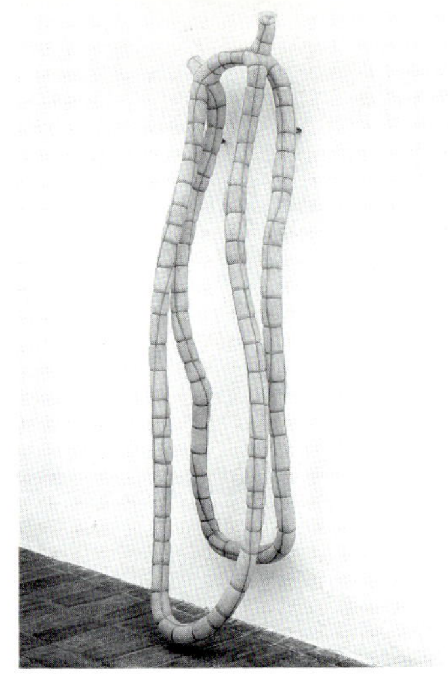

doublepoodleloopheader, 1991–92

CHECKLIST OF THE EXHIBITION

Studio Works

Except where noted, all works are from the collection of the artist, courtesy of L. A. Louver, Venice, California

bigheader, 1986–89
Steel
8 x 146 x 10½ in.
(20.3 x 370.8 x 26.7 cm)

blackmouthheader, 1987–89
Bronze
4½ x 283 x 8 in.
(11.4 x 718.8 x 20.3 cm)
Douglas S. Cramer Foundation
Figure 56

blackdress, 1990–91
Bronze
62 x 77 x 55 in.
(157.5 x 195.6 x 139.7 cm)
Private collection
Figure 4

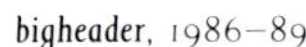

bigheader, 1986–89

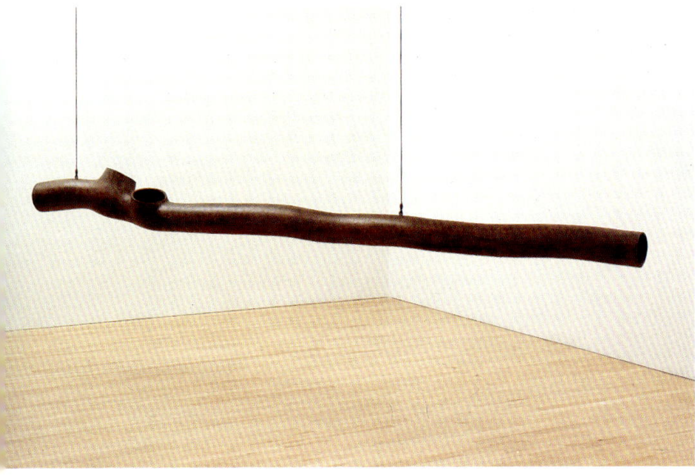

fourleg, 1990–91
Bronze
119 x 24 x 22 in.
(302.3 x 61.7 x 55.9 cm)
Private collection
Page 6

horseheader, 1990–91
Bronze
62 x 148 x 48 in.
(157.5 x 375.9 x 121.9 cm)
Figure 52 and back cover

nightymonster, 1990–91
Bronze
132 x 32 x 24 in.
(335.3 x 81.3 x 61 cm)
Figure 6

snakearm, 1990–91
Bronze
71 x 244 x 12 in.
(180.3 x 619.8 x 30.5 cm)
Collection of Kenneth and Judy Dayton
Figures 2–3

u-bone with drain, 1990–92
Mixed media
78 x 48 x 8 in.
(198.1 x 121.9 x 20.3 cm)
Figure 57

knifeedge, 1990–93
Mixed media
87 x 35 x 8 in.
(221 x 88.9 x 20.3 cm)
Private collection, courtesy of L.A. Louver

udderheader, 1990–93
Bronze
66 x 123½ x 26 in.
(167.6 x 313.7 x 66 cm)

birthbone, 1991–92
Mixed media
115 x 19 x 7½ in.
(292.1 x 48.2 x 19.1 cm)
Collection of Sharon Takeda and Peter Shelton

doublepoodleloopheader, 1991–92
Mixed media
91 x 24½ x 18 in.
(231.1 x 54.6 x 45.7 cm)

broadwing, 1991–93
Mixed media
48 x 69 x 22½ in.
(121.9 x 175.3 x 57.2 cm)

bigfootbottle, 1992–93
Mixed media
87 x 28 x 25 in.
(221 x 71.1 x 63.5 cm)

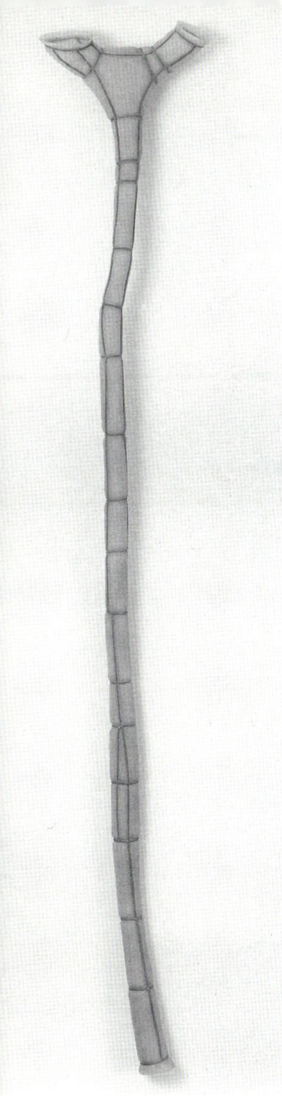

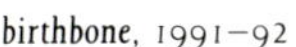
birthbone, 1991–92

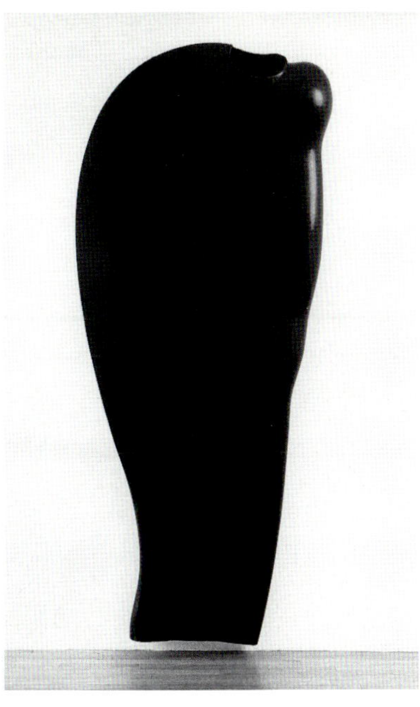

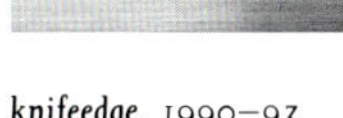
knifeedge, 1990–93

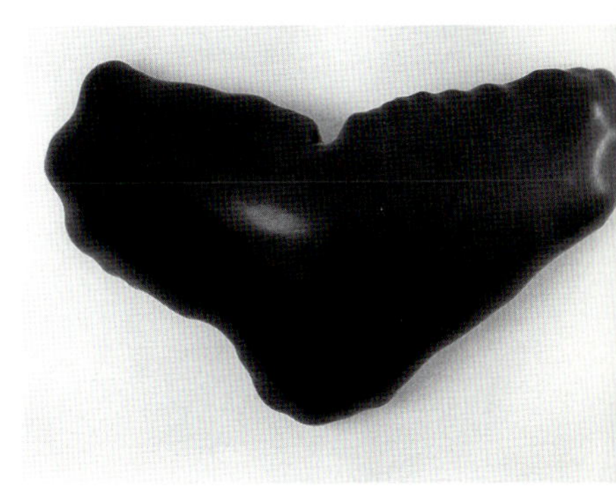

broadwing, 1991–93

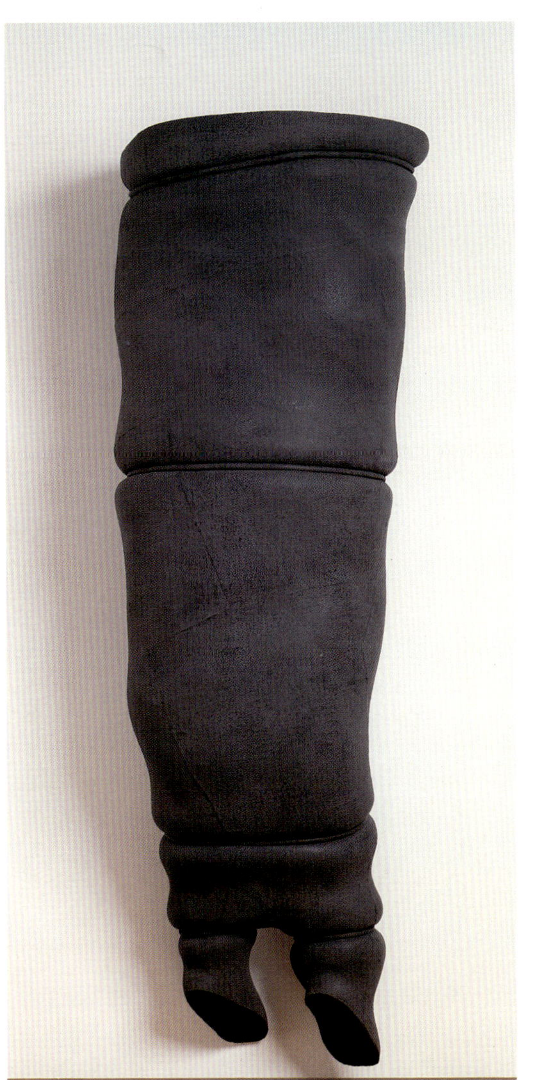

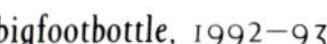
bigfootbottle, 1992–93

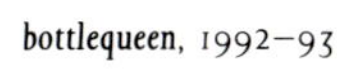
bottlequeen, 1992–93

bottlequeen, 1992–93
Mixed media
60 x 21 x 30 in.
(152.4 x 53.3 x 76.2 cm)

bulgebone, 1992–93
Mixed media
65 x 15 x 26¾ in.
(165.1 x 38.1 x 67.9 cm)
Allen Memorial Art Museum, Oberlin College, Ohio; Roush Fund for Contemporary Art and gift of John N. Stern (oc '39) in honor of the artist's parents, David and Mary McCullough Shelton (oc '37/'36), and in memory of their good friend Robert S. Hunt (oc '39), 1993

whitebagbone, 1992–93
Mixed media
75 x 13½ x 15 in.
(190.5 x 34.3 x 38.1 cm)

cannonbottle, 1992–94
Bronze
68 x 56 x 32 in.
(172.7 x 142.2 x 81.3 cm)
Page 72

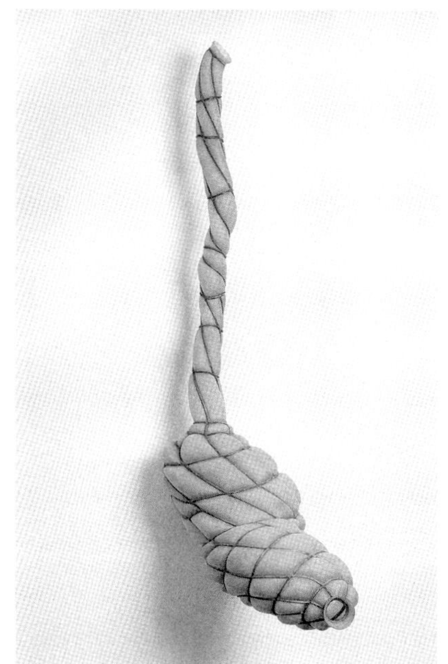
bulgebone, 1992–93

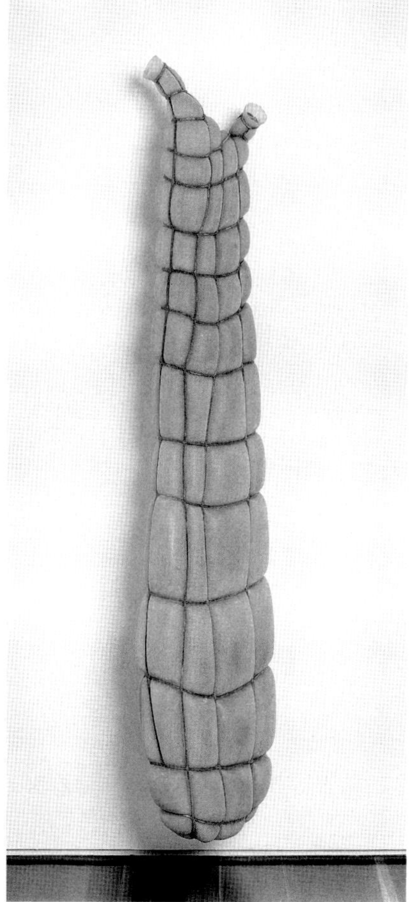
whitebagbone, 1992–93

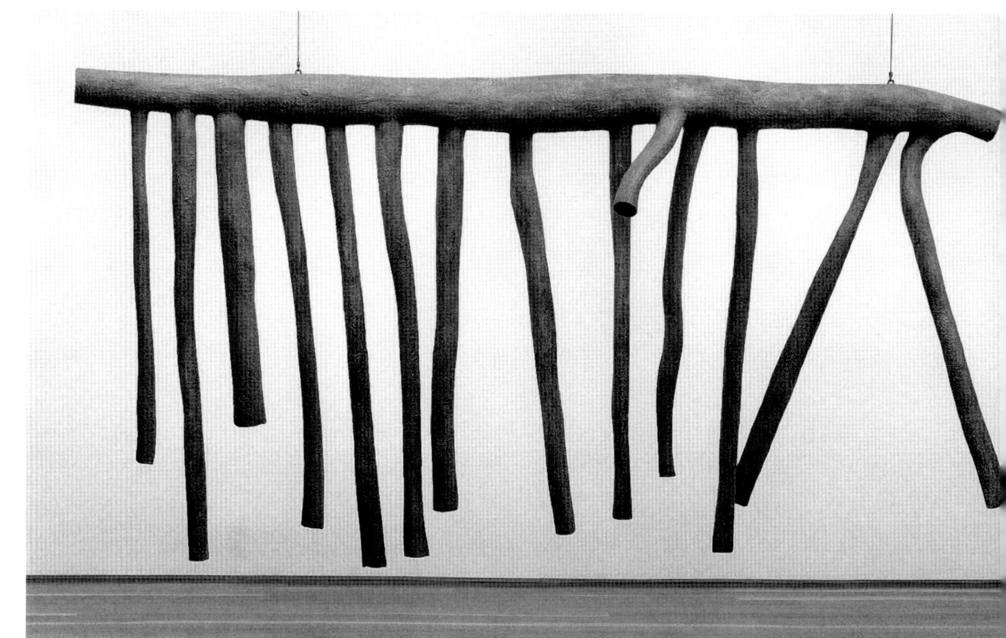
udderheader, 1990–93

boots (detail), 1989

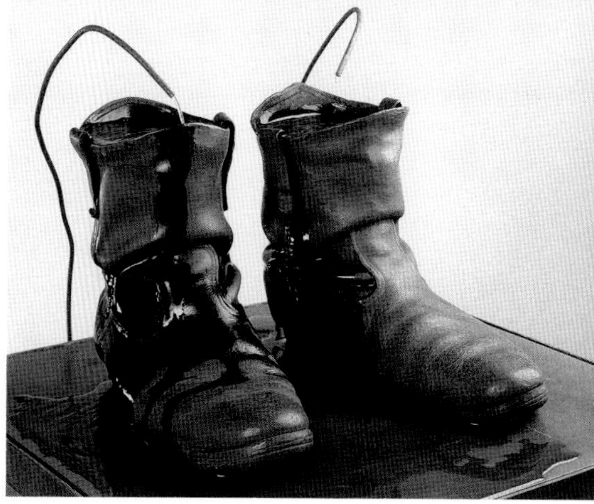

Individual Works from
thingsgetwet, 1989–94
Total dimensions variable

boots, 1989
Bronze, water, copper, pump, and wood
15 x 22 x 22 in.
(38.1 x 55.9 x 55.9 cm)

brain, 1989
Bronze, water, copper, and pump
69 x 17 x 16 in.
(175.3 x 43.2 x 40.6 cm)
Page 10 and figure 46

waterbaby, 1989
Bronze, water, copper, pump, and wood
11½ x 20 x 16 in.
(29.2 x 50.8 x 40.6 cm)

blanket, 1993
Bronze, water, copper, pump, and wood
41 x 32 x 28 in.
(106.7 x 81.3 x 71.1 cm)
Figure 49

books, 1993
Bronze, water, copper, pump, and wood
65 x 18 x 18 in.
(165.1 x 45.7 x 45.7 cm)
Front cover and figures 44–45

bowlshutch, 1993
Bronze, water, copper, and pump
69 x 35 x 34 in.
(175.3 x 88.9 x 86.4 cm)
Frontispiece and figures 40–41

breadwaterwall, 1993
Bronze, water, copper, pump, and wood
51 x 62½ x 18 in.
(129.5 x 158.8 x 45.7 cm)

churchsnakebedbone, 1993
Bronze, water, copper, and pumps
80 x 77 x 38 in.
(203.2 x 195.6 x 96.5 cm)
Figures 28–29

hammerspears, 1993
Bronze, water, copper, and pump
57 x 16 x 14 in.
(144.8 x 40.6 x 35.6 cm)

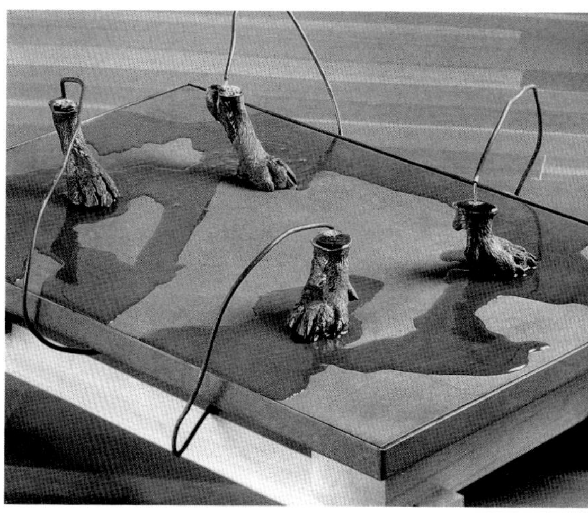

paws, 1993

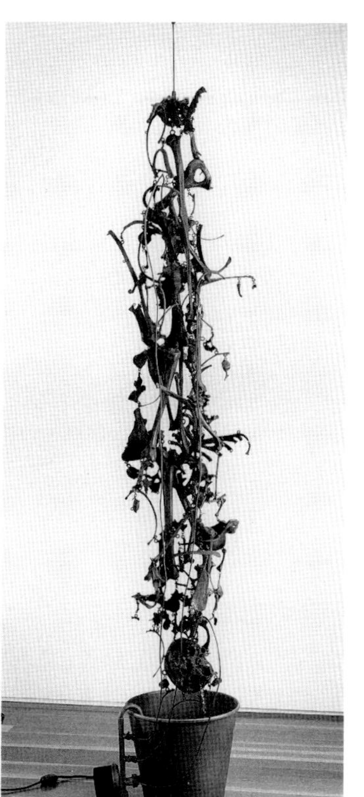

mandogbones, 1993

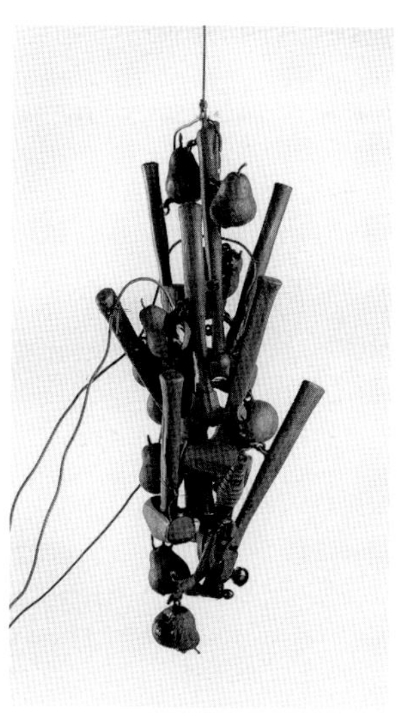

hammerspears (detail), 1993

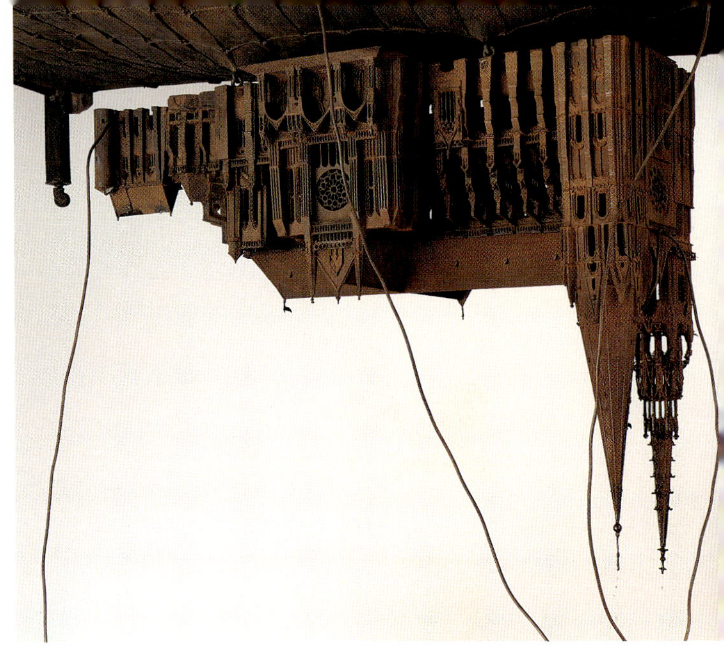

househeart, 1993
Bronze, water, copper, and pump
$65\frac{1}{2}$ x 16 x 14 in.
(166.4 x 40.6 x 35.6 cm)
Collection of Sharon Takeda and Peter Shelton

log, 1993
Bronze, water, copper, pump, and wood
44 x 30 x 20 in.
(111.8 x 76.2 x 50.8 cm)
Figure 50

mandogbones, 1993
Bronze, water, copper, and pump
86 x 18 x 19 in.
(218.4 x 45.7 x 48.3 cm)

oldwetbrickhouse, 1993
Bronze, water, copper, and pump
36 x 42 x 42 in.
(91.4 x 106.7 x 106.7 cm)
Figures 36 and 38

pagodawindowskull, 1993
Bronze, water, copper, pump, and wood
68 x 16 x 16 in.
(172.7 x 40.6 x 40.6 cm)
Figures 30–32

paws, 1993
Bronze, water, copper, pump, and wood
13 x $30\frac{1}{2}$ x 20 in.
(33 x 77.5 x 50.8 cm)

shotguncanetree, 1993
Bronze, water, copper, and pump
76 x 27 x 21 in.
(193 x 68.6 x 53.3 cm)
Figures 33–35

waterchair, 1993
Bronze, water, copper, pump, and wood
36 x 26 x 26 in.
(91.4 x 66 x 66 cm)
Figure 48

wetteeth, 1993
Bronze, water, copper, pump, and wood
36 x 30 x $19\frac{1}{2}$ in.
(91.4 x 76.2 x 49.5 cm)
Figure 25

littlepipes, 1993–94
Bronze, water, copper, pump, and wood
$38\frac{1}{2}$ x $93\frac{1}{2}$ x 16 in.
(97.8 x 237.5 x 40.6 cm)

romandrain, 1993–94
Bronze, water, copper, and pumps
$58\frac{1}{2}$ x 23 x $34\frac{1}{2}$ in.
(148.6 x 58.4 x 87.6 cm)

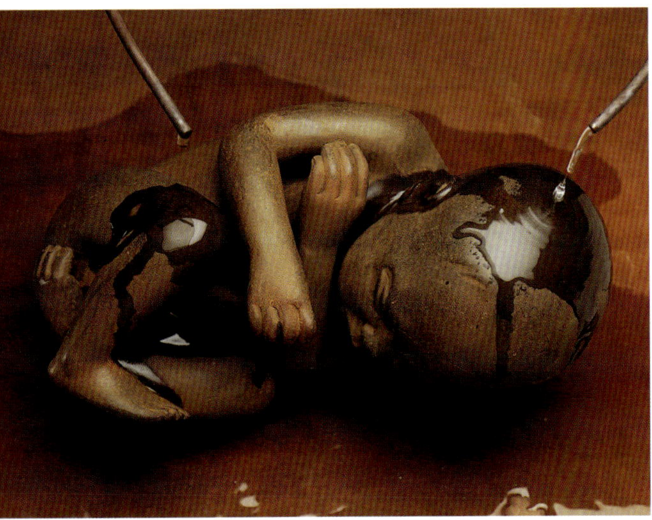

waterbaby (detail), 1989

churchsnakebedbone (detail), 1993

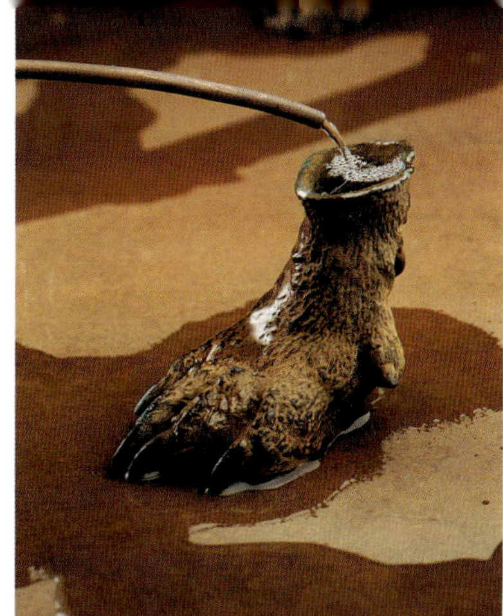

paws (detail), 1993

mandogbones (detail), 1993

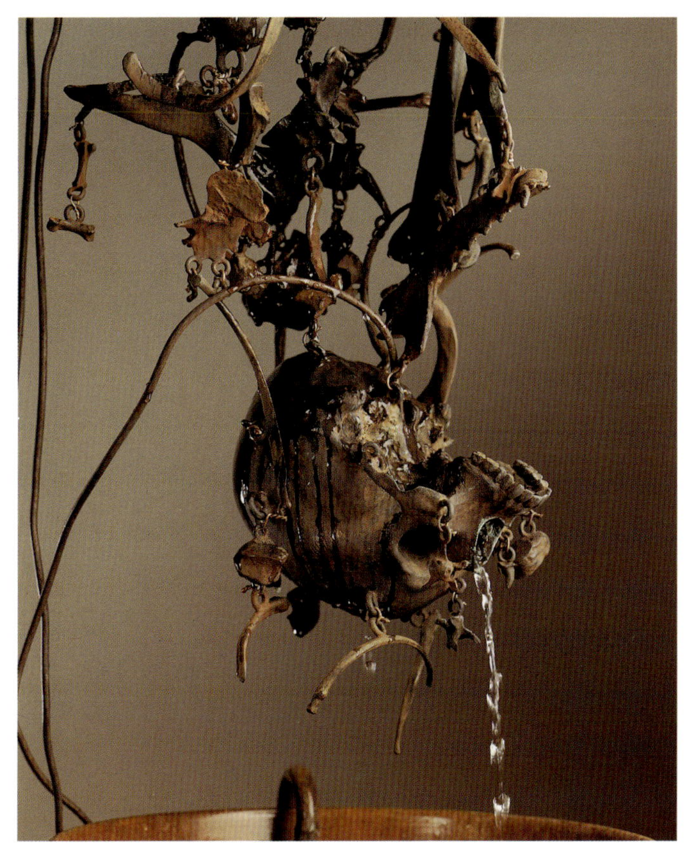

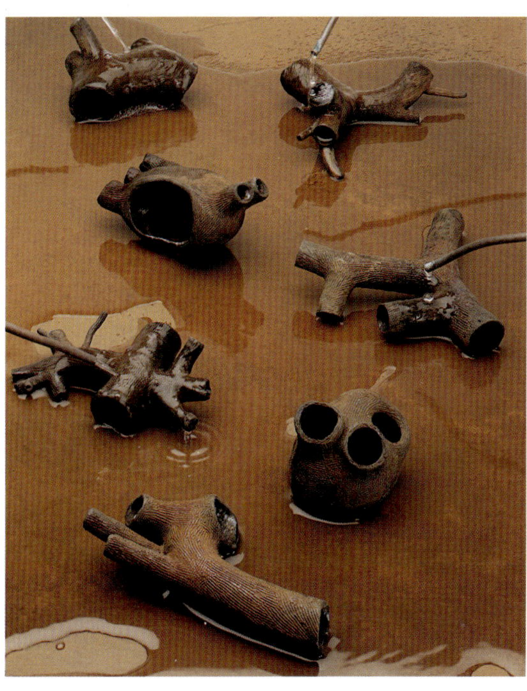

littlepipes (detail), 1993–94

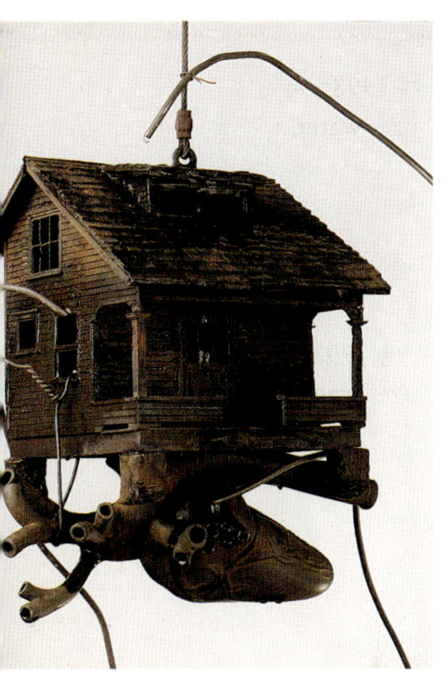

househeart (detail), 1993

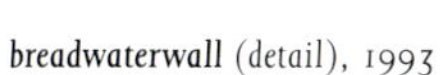

breadwaterwall (detail), 1993

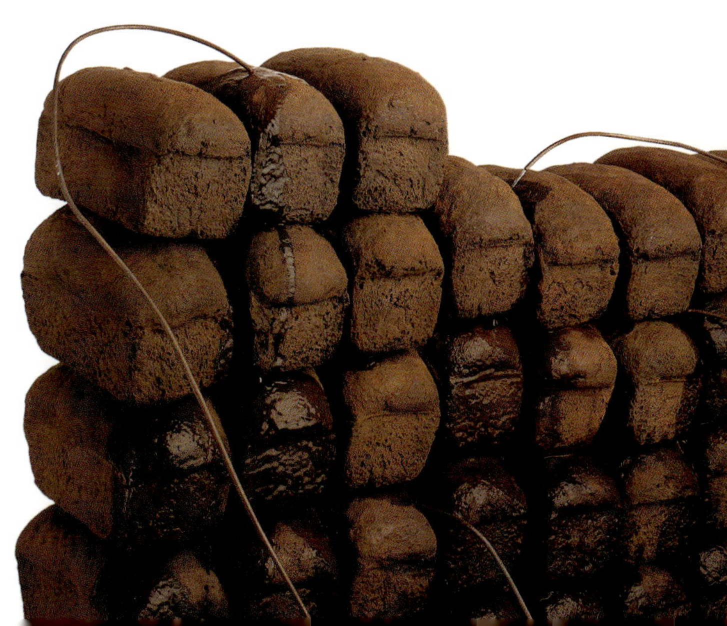

BIOGRAPHY

1951 born Troy, Ohio, 18 January

1973 receives B.A. from Pomona College, Claremont, California

1974 receives trade certifications from Hobart Brothers School of Welding Technology, Troy, Ohio; moves to Los Angeles

1977 receives Purchase Award, Art in Public Places Exhibition, Cheney Cowles Memorial Art Museum, Spokane, Washington

1979 receives M.F.A. from University of California, Los Angeles

1980, 1982, 1984
receives National Endowment for the Arts Individual Artist Fellowships

1985 receives Young Talent Award, Los Angeles County Museum of Art

1987 receives Louis Comfort Tiffany Foundation Fellowship

1989 receives John Simon Guggenheim Memorial Foundation Fellowship

lives and works in Los Angeles

EXHIBITION HISTORY

Solo Exhibitions

1979

Wight Art Gallery, University of California, Los Angeles. SWEATHOUSE *and little principals* (111-element version). June 17–July 1.

1980

Los Angeles Contemporary Exhibitions. BROWNROOMS 1977–78. June 4–28.

Artpark, Lewiston, New York. HEADROOM *footspace.* July 1980–September 1985. Exh. cat.

Chapman College, Orange, California. BIRDHOUSE *holecan.* October 18–November 26. Exh. cat., *Architectural Sculpture: Installations*, by Richard Turner.

1981

Malinda Wyatt Gallery, Venice, California. NECKWALL *footscreen, sleeper.* April 25–June 27.

1982

Open Space Gallery, Victoria, British Columbia. *trunknuts,* WHITEHEAD, *floater.* June 29–August 7. Exh. cat. by Christopher Knight.

Santa Barbara Contemporary Arts Forum. SWEATHOUSE *and little principals* (150-element version). November 7–December 3.

Artists Space, New York City. *white, round,* HEAD. December 11–January 15, 1983.

1984

L.A. Louver and Malinda Wyatt Gallery, Venice, California. MAJORJOINTS, *hangers and squat.* March 15–April 14.

Portland Center for the Visual Arts, Oregon. *pipegut, waterseat and* STANDSTILL. April 27–June 2. Exh. cat. by Brian O'Douherty.

1986

University of Massachusetts, Amherst. *floatinghouse* DEADMAN. February 1–March 16. Itinerary: Wight Art Gallery, University of California, Los Angeles, February 3–March 8, 1987; Herron Gallery, Indianapolis Center for Contemporary Art, March 18–April 29, 1989; Louver Gallery, New York City, January 6–February 3, 1990. Exh. cat. by Peter Shelton, with excerpts from an interview by Helaine Posner.

L.A. Louver, Venice, California. *Peter Shelton: Recent Sculptures.* November 28–December 27.

1988

Des Moines Art Center. *Peter Shelton: Waxworks.* September 24–November 13. Itinerary: San Jose Museum of Art, February 28–March 26, 1989; La Jolla Museum of Contemporary Art, April 7–June 4, 1989. Exh. cat. by Cornelia H. Butler.

1989

L.A. Louver, Venice, California. *Peter Shelton: Castings*. May 27–June 24.

Fine Arts Gallery, University of California, Irvine. *bag*, BOX TUB, *tubes and pipes*. November 14–December 10.

1990

L.A. Louver, Venice, California. *Peter Shelton: Drawings*. August 11–September 8.

1991

Louver Gallery, New York City. *Peter Shelton: Sculptures*. February 9–March 9.

L.A. Louver, Venice, California. *monstermawbaggutheaderhead and shirts*. December 7–January 4, 1992.

1992

Sperone Gallery, Rome. *Peter Shelton*. March 23–April 19.

Allen Memorial Art Museum, Oberlin College, Ohio. *Peter Shelton*. May 23–July 12.

Faith and Charity in Hope Gallery, Hope, Idaho. *Peter Shelton*. August 5–September 5. Exh. cat. by Edward Kienholz.

Arts Club of Chicago. *Peter Shelton: Drawings and Sculptures*. November 16–January 2, 1993. Exh. cat. by Carol S. Eliel.

1993

Louver Gallery, New York City. *thingsgetwet*. May 1–June 5.

Group Exhibitions

1977

Cheney Cowles Memorial Museum, Spokane. *Art in Public Places*. October 1–31. Exh. cat.

1980

College of Art, The Maryland Institute, Baltimore. *Sculpture 1980*. June 3–26. Exh. cat.

Los Angeles Municipal Art Gallery. *Architectural Sculpture*. September 30–October 28.

Los Angeles Institute of Contemporary Art. *Architectural Sculpture*. September 30–November 21. Exh. cats., *Architectural Scupture: History and Documents*, by Lucy Lippard and *Architectural Sculpture: Installations*, by Richard Turner.

1981

Libra Gallery, Claremont Graduate School of Fine Arts, California. *Divola, Picot, Shelton*. September 25–October 9.

Downtown Gallery, Los Angeles. *The Intimate Object*. November 15–December 24.

1982

Musée d'Art Moderne de la Ville de Paris. *Une expérience muséographique: Échange entre artistes 1931–1982 Pologne-U.S.A.* June 25–September 6. Itinerary: Ulster Museum, Belfast, January 20–February 20, 1983; Douglas Hyde Gallery, University of Dublin, March 25–April 30, 1983; Museum Stuki, Lodz, Poland, permanent installation. Exh. cat.

Fresno Art Center and Museum. *Forgotten Dimensions: A Survey of Small Sculpture in California Now*. September 15–November 15. Exh. cat. by Roger Bolomey.

1983

Center on Contemporary Art, Seattle. *Public Comments*. December 3–January 28, 1984.

1984

College of Creative Studies, University of California, Santa Barbara. *Constructed Metal: Modern Sculpture*. January 10–February 10. Exh. cat. by Francis Colpitt.

The Venice Biennale. *Aperto '84*. June 10–September 9. Exh. cat. by Flavio Caroli.

L.A. Louver, Venice, California. *Paintings, Drawings and Sculptures. American and European*. July 20–September 22.

Fine Arts Gallery, University of California, Irvine. *Selections from the Merry and Bill Norris Collection*. October 11–November 3. Exh. cat. by Melinda Wortz.

1985

Galleria Comunale d'Arte Moderna, Bologna. *Anniottanta*. July 4–September 30. Exh. cat. by Giacinto di Pietrantonio.

L.A. Louver, Venice, California. *American and European Painting and Sculpture. Part 1*. July 16–August 17.

Claremont Graduate School of Fine Arts, California. *Art Out*. September 16–October 4.

1986

L.A. Louver, Venice, California. *Sculptures and Drawings by Sculptors*. April 4–26.

1987

Palm Springs Desert Museum. *California Figurative Sculpture*. January 30–March 15. Exh. cat. by Michael Zakian.

Los Angeles County Museum of Art. *Avant-Garde in the Eighties*. April 23–July 12. Exh. cat. by Howard N. Fox.

Curt Marcus Gallery, New York City. *Invitational Exhibition*. May 29–July 3.

Goldie Paley Gallery, Moore College of Art, Philadelphia. *Bronze Plaster & Polyester*. November 16–December 12.

Whitney Museum of American Art at Philip Morris, New York City. *Elements: Five Installations*. December 17–January 27, 1988. Exh. cat. by Kathleen Monaghan.

Lannan Museum, Lake Worth, Florida. *Abstract Expressions: Recent Sculpture*. December 18–May 10, 1988. Exh. cat. by Bonnie Clearwater.

1988

Montgomery Gallery, Pomona College, Claremont, California. *Pomona College Alumni Artists: A Centennial Exhibition*. March 6–April 17.

Museum of Contemporary Art, Los Angeles. *Striking Distance.* March 22–June 19. Itinerary: Triton Museum, Santa Clara, California, July 16–August 28; Fresno Art Center and Museum, September 17–October 30; University Art Gallery, Sonoma State University, Rohnert Park, California, November 17–December 16.

Walker Art Center, Minneapolis. *Sculpture Inside Outside.* May 22–September 18. Itinerary: Houston Museum of Fine Arts, December 10–March 5, 1989. Exh. cat.

Main Art Gallery, Visual Arts Center, California State University, Fullerton. *Models: Handheld Ideas.* November 5–December 2. Exh. cat. by Christopher D. Byal.

Fisher Gallery, University of Southern California, Los Angeles. *Sculture da camera, Chamber Sculptures.* November 28–January 11, 1989. Exh. cat.

1989

Security Pacific Gallery, Costa Mesa, California. *Art in the Public Eye: Selected Developments.* June 13–August 19. Exh. cat.

Museum of Contemporary Art, Los Angeles. *Constructing a History: A Focus on the Permanent Collection.* November 19–March 4, 1990.

1990

Louver Gallery, New York City. *Territory of Desire.* February 17–March 10.

Armory Center for the Arts, Pasadena. *Selections from the Carnation Company Collection.* May 31–July 8.

L.A. Louver, Venice, California. *Sculptors' Drawings.* June 2–30.

San Diego Museum of Contemporary Art, La Jolla. *Selections from the Permanent Collection.* Itinerary: Duke University Museum of Art, Durham, September 7–November 4; J. B. Speed Art Museum, Louisville, December 4–January 27, 1991; Springfield Museum of Fine Arts, Massachusetts, March 3–May 19, 1991; San Diego Museum of Contemporary Art, June 8–August 4, 1991; Memorial Art Gallery of the University of Rochester, New York, September 28–November 17, 1991; Utah Museum of Fine Arts, University of Utah, Salt Lake City, May 18–June 28, 1992; Philbrook Museum of Art, Tulsa, July 17–September 1, 1992. Exh. cat. by Ronald J. Onorato.

Santa Barbara Contemporary Arts Forum. *Spirit of Our Time.* November 6–December 27.

1991

California State University, Bakersfield. *L.A. 1990: Selected Views.* January 24–February 24.

Sezon Museum of Art, Tokyo. *Individual Realities in the California Art Scene.* May 11–June 10. Itinerary: Seibu Tsukashin Hall, Amagasaki, June 15–July 22. Exh. cat. by Tetsuro Shimizu.

San Diego Museum of Contemporary Art, La Jolla. *The Artist's Hand: Drawings from the Bank of America Art Collection.* June 7–August 4.

1992

Museum of Contemporary Art, Los Angeles. *Recent Acquisitions: Selected New Works in the Permanent Collection.* February 9–May 17.

Museum of Modern Art, New York City. *Contemporary Works from the Collection.* March 5–July 22.

Museo Cantonale d'Arte, Lugano. *Panza di Biumo: The Eighties and the Nineties from the Collection*. April 10–July 5. Exh. cat. by Manuela Kahn-Rossi.

Los Angeles Municipal Art Gallery. *LAX: The Los Angeles Exhibition*. December 5–January 24, 1993. Exh. cat.

1993

Louver Gallery, New York City. *Mol, Nash, Shelton*. January 9–February 6.

Frankfurter Kunstverein, Frankfurt. *Prospectus 1993*. March 20–May 23. Exh. cat.

Main Art Gallery, California State University, Fullerton. *Elegant, Irreverent & Obsessive: Drawing in Southern California*. April 17–May 16. Itinerary: Dorothy Goldeen Gallery, Santa Monica, California, May 29–July 10. Exh. cat.

SELECTED BIBLIOGRAPHY

1979

Julie, K.C. *Peter Shelton—SWEATHOUSE and little principals.* Los Angeles: Helicon Video.

1980

Fahr, Barry. "Enigmatic Architecture." *Artweek* 11, no. 23, 21 June, 5.

Larson, Kay. "Is There a Crimp in the Beauty Parlor?" *Village Voice*, 10 September, 77.

Muchnic, Suzanne. "Sprawling Sculptures." *Los Angeles Times*, 2 November, "Calendar" 90.

Brodhead, Wendy. "Protection and Entrapment." *Artweek* 11, no. 39, 22 November, 4.

1981

Drohojowska, Hunter. "Peter Shelton." *L.A. Weekly*, 1 May, 62.

Pincus, Robert L. "Peter Shelton." *Los Angeles Times*, 1 May, sect. 6, 7–8.

Knight, Christopher. "Your Place or Shelton's." *Los Angeles Herald Examiner*, 10 May, E3.

Blaine, Michael. "Formalist Shelter." *Artweek* 12, no. 18, 16 May, 6.

Schipper, Merle. "Peter Shelton's Places and Spaces." *Images and Issues* 1, no. 4 (spring): 24–25.

Perreault, John. "Park's Lot." *Soho Weekly News*, 25 August, 23.

Wortz, Melinda. "A Tropical Sleeper." *ArtNews* 80, no. 8 (October): 189.

Lewison, David. "Nebulae of Color." *Artweek* 12, no. 37, 7 November, 6.

1982

Harwig, Michael R. "Peter Shelton." In *The List*. 6th ed. New York: Independent Curators Incorporated.

Wright, Patricia. "Forum—Museums and Galleries." *Domus*, no. 627 (April): 77.

Wilson, Raymond L. "Small Metaphors." *Artweek* 13, no. 17, 1 May, 4.

Shelton, Peter. "NECKWALL, footscreen, sleeper." *Dreamworks* 2, no. 3, (spring): 203–7.

Amos, Robert. "Peter Shelton at Open Space Gallery." *Vanguard* 11 (October/November): 27–28.

Timberman, Marcy. "Peter Shelton: The Power of the Ordinary." *Artweek* 13, no. 40, 27 November, 1, 16.

1983

Hicks, Mary. "Peter Shelton." *Images and Issues* 3, no. 5 (March/April): 63–64.

Wortz, Melinda. "Peter Shelton—Contemporary Arts Forum, Santa Barbara: SWEATHOUSE and little principals 1977–82." *ArtNews* 82, no. 5 (May): 133–36.

Hackett, Regina. "Public Comments." *Seattle Post-Intelligencer*, 7 December, C12.

Smallwood, Lyn. "COCA's 'Public Comments': An Old Warehouse for New Art." *Weekly* (Seattle), 7 December, 40–41.

1984

Schipper, Merle. "Plausible Dream," *Arts and Architecture* 3, no. 2, (2d quarter): 15–16.

Pincus, Robert L. "Peter Shelton." *Los Angeles Times*, 23 March, sect. 6, 14.

Glowen, Ron. "Morphology and Material." *Artweek* 15, no. 21, 26 May, 5.

Gardner, Colin. "Peter Shelton at L.A. Louver and Malinda Wyatt Galleries." *Images and Issues* 5, no. 1 (July/August): 41.

Panza di Biumo, Giuseppe. "La Biennale." *Domus*, no. 652 (August): 72. In Italian.

Gendel, Milton. "Report from Venice: Cultured Pearls at the Biennale." *Art in America* 72, no. 8 (September): 51.

Groot, Paul. "Closed Quotes." *Artforum* 23, no. 1 (September): 107.

1985

Muchnic, Suzanne. "2 Sculptors Earn Young Talent Prize." *Los Angeles Times*, 14 June, "Calendar" 1, 5.

Rico, Diana. "Young Talent Gets Award, Showing from Museum." *Daily News* (Los Angeles), 24 June, "Life" 21.

Drohojowska, Hunter. "The Prize." *Los Angeles Herald Examiner*, 25 June, C3.

Bodino, Maristella di. "I Dopotutto." *Epoca* (Milan), 19 July, 42–51. In Italian.

Cabutti, Lucio. "Uno sguardo sugli anni ottanta—Bologna e altre città." *Arte* 15, no. 154 (July/August): 26. In Italian.

1986

Holland, Laura. "Peter Shelton: University of Massachusetts, Amherst." *Art New England* 7, no. 3 (March): 10.

Artner, Alan G. "What's New in Art? 20 Insiders Tell Who's Hot—and Why." *Chicago Tribune*, 29 June, sect. 13, 26, 29.

McKenna, Kristine. "Peter Shelton." *Los Angeles Times*, 5 December, sect. 6, 11–14.

1987

Conrad, Barnaby. "Los Angeles: The New Mecca." *Horizon* 30, no. 1 (January/February): 30.

Mallinson, Constance. "Peter Shelton." *Art in America* 75, no. 2 (February): 154–55.

Knight, Christopher. "'DEADMAN' Exhibit Exudes Life." *Los Angeles Herald Examiner*, 26 February, B7.

Bulmer, Marge. "Peter Shelton." *Reader*, Los Angeles, 27 February, 21.

Anderson, Michael. "Peter Shelton." *L.A. Weekly*, 27 February, 121.

Bijvoet, Marga. "Engaging the Viewer/Participant." *Artweek* 18, no. 8, 28 February, 1.

Muchnic, Suzanne. "Exploring a House That Floats." *Los Angeles Times*, 2 March, sect. 6, 1, 3.

Muchnic, Suzanne. "The Way We Are Figuratively." *Los Angeles Times*, 3 March, "Calendar" 1, 4.

Baltierra, Miguel. "floatinghouse DEADMAN." *L.A. Architect* (March): 6–7.

Gardner, Colin. "Peter Shelton." *Artforum* 25, no. 9 (May): 158.

Drohojowska, Hunter. "The Artists Who Matter: L.A.'s New Scene Makes History." *Antiques and Fine Art* 4, no. 4 (May/June): 49–55.

Clothier, Peter. "Peter Shelton: Dwellings in the Abstract." *ArtNews* 86, no. 7 (September): 83–84.

1988

The Louis Comfort Tiffany Foundation: Awards in Painting, Sculpture, Printmaking, and Craft Media. New York: The Louis Comfort Tiffany Foundation.

Friedman, Martin. "Growing the Garden." *Design Quarterly*, no. 141 (winter): 41.

Levin, Kim. "Art Walk." *Village Voice*, 5 January, 84.

Brenson, Michael. "A Transient Art Form with Staying Power." *New York Times*, 10 January, H33, H36.

Brenson, Michael. "Art: From Robert Morris." *New York Times*, 15 January, C23.

Brenson, Michael. "Fossilization Evolves into a Modern Metaphor." *New York Times*, 31 January, H31, H33.

Knight, Christopher. "Contemporary Art Concerns." *Los Angeles Herald Examiner*, 3 April, F4.

Martin, Mary Abbe. "Walker's Sculpture Show Provocative, Grand in Scale." *Star Tribune* (Minneapolis), 27 May, 2E.

Muchnic, Suzanne. "Cohesive Show Looks at Life from Distance." *New Art Examiner* 15, no. 10 (June): 33–35.

Raczka, Robert. "MOCA Sights Local Art in 'Striking Distance.'" *New Art Examiner* 15, no. 10 (June): 39–40.

Rand, David. "Aesthetic Anarchy: The Walker Art Center Turns Contemporary Sculpture Inside Out in an Exuberant Exhibition." *Horizon* 31, no. 5 (June): 33–35.

Brenson, Michael. "Coming to Grips with Contemporary Sculpture." *New York Times*, 19 June, sect. 2, 33.

Nussbaum, Eliot. "Shelton 'Floats' His Sculpture Show." *Des Moines Sunday Register*, 2 October, 8F.

Johnson, Patricia C. "Sculpture Isn't Always What It Seems To Be." *Houston Chronicle*, 7 December, D1, D3.

1989

Riddle, Mason. "A Modernist Museum without Walls." *New Art Examiner* 16, no. 5 (January): 36–37.

Burkhart, Dorothy. "San Jose Museum Strikes a Balance." *San Jose Mercury News*, 24 February, E12.

Deragon, Rick. "Equivocal, Provocative Form." *Artweek* 20, no. 10, 11 March, 4.

Mannweiler, David. "House Seems to Float." *Indianapolis News*, 13 March, C1.

Baker, Kenneth. "Seductive Sculpture in San Jose." *San Francisco Chronicle*, 16 March, E5.

Mannheimer, Steve. "Artist's Installation Combats Weightiness." *Indianapolis Star*, 19 March, E12.

Garmel, Marion. "Life's Insecurity Revealed in floatinghouse's Halls." *Indianapolis News*, 23 March, D2.

Knight, Christopher.
"Shelton's Sculptural Delights." *Los Angeles Herald Examiner*, 23 April, E2.

Pincus, Robert L.
"In 'Waxworks' Body Parts Make a Whole Exhibit." *San Diego Union*, 23 April, E1, E4.

Timberman, Marcy.
"The Body Language of Peter Shelton." *Galeries Magazine*, no. 30 (April/May): 76–77.

Curtis, Cathy.
"Peter Shelton's Eccentric Shapes at La Jolla." *Los Angeles Times*, 4 May, sect. 6, 12.

Curtis, Cathy.
"Venice: The Galleries." *Los Angeles Times*, 2 June, sect. 6, 16.

Curtis, Cathy.
"Security Pacific Banks on a New Gallery." *Los Angeles Times*, 13 June, sect. 6, 4.

Morgan, Stuart.
"Past Present Future—Count Giuseppe Panza di Biumo Interviewed." *Artscribe*, no. 76 (summer): 56.

Stephens, Richard.
"Peter Shelton: Waxworks." *New Art Examiner* 16, no. 11 (summer): 48.

Calhoon, Sharon.
"Peter Shelton." *Dialogue* 12, no. 4 (July/August): 2, 30.

Tedeschi, Pierparide.
"The Panza di Biumo Collection," *Contemporanea* 74, no. 10 (September): 48–55. In Italian.

Ballatore, Sandy.
"The Body Architecture of Peter Shelton." *Artspace* 13, no. 3 (September/October): 52–57.

Britton, Donald.
"Peter Shelton." *Art Issues*, no. 6 (September/October): 26.

Princenthal, Nancy.
"The Body in Question." *Sculpture* 8, no. 5 (September/October): 24–29.

Curtis, Cathy.
"Simple Sculpture Exhibit Fills Austere Surroundings with Bold Presence." *Los Angeles Times*, 20 November, F3.

Clothier, Peter.
"L.A. Outward Bound." *ArtNews* 88, no. 10 (December): 130.

Pincus, Robert L.
"1989: The State of the Arts." *San Diego Union*, 28 December, E5.

1990

Smith, Roberta.
"Fresh, Hot and Headed for Fame: These Are the Faces to Watch." *New York Times*, 5 January, B7.

Larson, Kay.
"Upon Reflection." *New York* 23, no. 4 (29 January): 60.

Levin, Kim.
"Peter Shelton, Louver Gallery." *Village Voice*, 30 January, 93.

Johnson, Ken.
"Peter Shelton at Louver." *Art in America* 78, no. 3 (March): 196–97.

Mahoney, Robert.
"Peter Shelton—floatinghouse DEADMAN." *Arts Magazine* 64, no. 8 (April): 109.

Kalina, Richard.
"Peter Shelton—Louver Gallery." *Tema Celeste*, no. 25 (April/June): 68–69.

Heartney, Eleanor.
"New York." *Contemporanea* 74, no. 18 (May): 55.

Melrod, George.
"Peter Shelton—Louver Gallery New York." *Contemporanea* 74, no. 18 (May): 98. In Italian.

Zeichner, Arlene.
"L.A. Louver's Soho Gamble." *L.A. Style* (June): 62.

Kachur, Lewis.
"New York: Revivals and Survivals." *Art International*, no. 11 (summer): 71.

Snow, Shauna.
"The Scene: Peter Shelton Drawings at L.A. Louver." *Los Angeles Times* 12 August, "Calendar" 102.

McKenna, Kristine.
"Bodywork: Peter Shelton." *Los Angeles Times*, 21 August, F4.

Whiteson, Leon.
"Artful Lodgings: Merry Norris's Canyon Retreat." *Angeles* (September): 101, 107, 162.

Shelton, Peter.
"kettlehouse ICEHOUSE ironhouse." *ZYZZYVA* 6, no. 3 (fall): 66–67.

Hammond, Pamela.
"Peter Shelton, L.A. Louver." *ArtNews* 89, no. 9 (November): 178–80.

1991

Beaumont, Mary Rose.
"New Directions in International Sculpture." In *New Art: An International Survey*. Edited by Andreas Papadakis, Claire Farrow, and Nicola Hodges. New York: Rizzoli International Publications, Inc.

Marks, Ben.
"Peter Shelton: Body Language." *Angeles* (January): 32–35.

Brenson, Michael.
"Peter Shelton." *New York Times*, 1 March, C25.

Decter, Joshua.
"Peter Shelton at Louver Gallery." *Arts Magazine* 65, no. 9 (May): 103.

Melrod, George.
"Peter Shelton, Louver." *ArtNews* 90, no. 5 (May): 149–50.

Kosenko, Peter.
"Peter Shelton at L.A. Louver." *Artweek* 22, no. 44, 26 December, 13–14.

Pagel, David.
"Shelton in Wonderland." *Los Angeles Times*, 26 December, F15.

1992

Ianco-Starrels, Josine.
Facets of the Gas Company Collection. Los Angeles: Southern California Gas Company.

Kandel, Susan.
"Peter Shelton." *Arts Magazine* 66, no. 7 (March): 88–89.

Barrie, Lita.
"On the Scene: Los Angeles." *Artspace* 16, no. 3, (May/June): 82.

Halpern, Nora Brougher.
"Peter Shelton at L.A. Louver." *Flash Art* 35, no. 164 (May/June): 117.

1993

Turner, Jonathan.
"The Berlingieris: A Nun, an Eskimo, and Elvis." *ArtNews* 92, no. 5 (May): 83–84, 86.

Levin, Kim.
"Voice Choices: Art." *Village Voice*, 15 June, 71.

Bourdon, David.
"Peter Shelton at Louver." *Art in America* 81, no. 9 (September): 112–13.

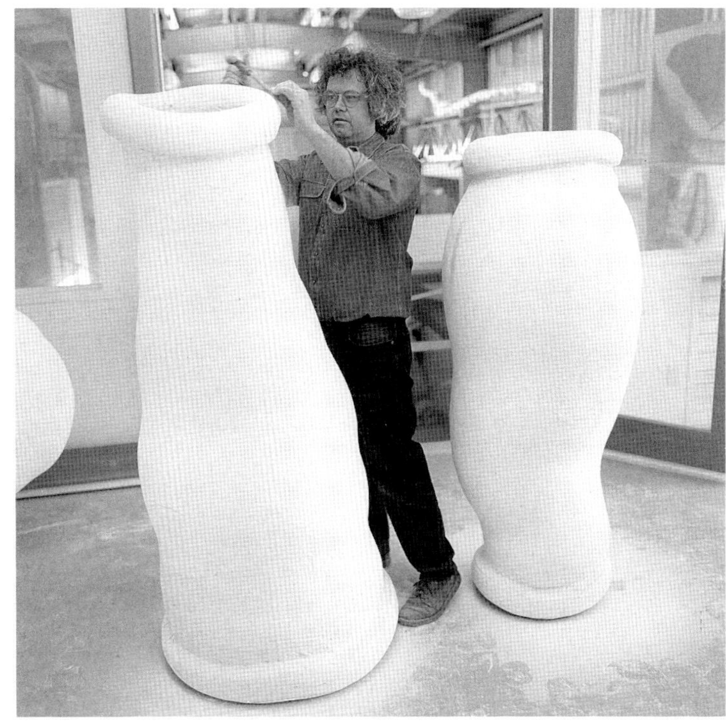

Peter Shelton in his studio with the plaster patterns for **cannonbottle**, December 1993.

EDITED BY MIYOSHI BAROSH

DESIGNED BY SCOTT TAYLOR

PHOTOGRAPHY BY JAY K. MCNALLY

COMPOSED IN MONOTYPE JOANNA AND SYNTAX

IMAGESETTING BY PREPRESS STUDIO, LOS ANGELES, CALIFORNIA

PRINTED BY TYPECRAFT, INC., PASADENA, CALIFORNIA